SINS

OF A

PRIEST

SINS

OF A

PRIEST

BRIAN ROBERT SMITH

3²³ooks

Toronto, Canada

Canadian Intellectual Property Office Registration Number: 1117588
Library of Congress Registration Number: TXu 1-572-236
ISBN (paperback first edition): 978-0-9920483-7-2

Published by 323 Books, Ontario, Canada

Cover Design by drmart.it
Male cover image copyright © 2014 Can Stock Photo Inc. / Bialasiewicz
Female cover image copyright © 2014 Gretchen Byers

Printed in the U. S. A.

DEDICATION

For my wife, Sonia.

To quote Bryan Adams, "Everything I do, I do it for you."

CHAPTER 1

ENGULFED IN COMPLETE DARKNESS, Father Burke sat while trying desperately to see the vigorous movement of something within a high ceiling. He realized he should have listened to his own warnings about coming here, especially at his age. He knew his time was running out, though, so he had no choice but to come. *If I can only hold on to it a little longer.*

A distant thunder rumbled and wood pounded. Ear shattering screeches resonated—like air escaping through splintered timber. Laughter echoed throughout the emptiness. This startled him and created a room so violated only he could find any sense being here. Suddenly, he turned sharply as lightning flashed through a stained glass window.

Just like so many times in the past, he was being played with. He knew the intention was for him to leave this place abandoned, but he simply couldn't do that. Invasions like this didn't scare him all that much, but not knowing if this would be the last was a terrifying thought to say the least.

He attempted to identify the intruder with an erratic flashlight beam that showed many rows of damaged church pews. Father Burke started moving. He struggled with a cane while he tried to make his way up the main aisle.

The light began to flicker. Frustrated, he banged it against his cane. Another bolt flashed. The flashlight dimmed.

He turned defeated, yet defiant. "Be damned, the soul of the devil."

CHAPTER 2

SITTING WITH ANOTHER MAN in the back of a bus, Marcus watched passengers rush toward the front. His immediate impulse was to join them, but he stayed put and looked out the window. Within a background of darkness, he only saw the highway they had been moving along, but now they were stopped. On the asphalt was the reflection of emergency lights flashing. It was a strong reminder about what he had been through in the past.

Many times, the same type of lights had prevented him from moving forward, just like now. This was supposed to be a new start for Marcus, but he was confused about the ultimate decision he'd made. It wasn't a question of if it was wrong for him, or if it would make him a better person. Those answers were clear. The problem was, would it make any difference? He stood and made his way slowly up the aisle knowing he wouldn't be going much further anytime soon.

Out the blood smeared front window, Marcus saw the mutilated carcass of a whitetail buck quivering in the middle of the illuminated road. He felt the presence of the other man watching from behind him. Judging by the thoughts going through Marcus's head, he probably would have been better off alone; but he had been riding with this man for quite some time, and it seemed appropriate to share at least some of what was on his mind. "Eight years ago, I felt as free as he did eight minutes ago," Marcus said with a shrug. "Luck's a survivor's greatest tool."

The man responded, "Was it luck that saved you?"

Marcus turned away from the window. He watched a bolt of lightning strike from a storm that violently assaulted the cityscape far off in the distance. "Back then, every day was just like that. Rain or shine, the storm never stopped." He rubbed his nose and looked away. Marcus noticed the man looking him over. *He's studying me—judging me. He's got an opinion already, over a few words. Well, maybe more than just words.* Marcus straightened the cuff of his black shirt and continued to smooth out the arm.

The man asked, "Drugs?"

Marcus started walking back toward his seat. "I was just a courier. What I delivered didn't matter."

"What did?"

Marcus sat down. Now he really wanted to be alone. "I guess I should be saying, forgive me, Father, for I have—, but that would be like pleading guilty before any charges were laid." He smiled at the man who now sat beside him. Marcus looked back out the front window. "You know, all that's in the past anyway. I used to think that when a man finds his path in life—his direction and purpose... Well, everything falls in line after that." He looked out the side window; at the storm. "I don't know..."

CHAPTER 3

DANIEL LEANED AGAINST A WALL of an alley. He was barely noticeable in the dark shadow he seemed part of. Lightning flashed his deep set and heavily weathered eyes. He closed them arrogantly and looked away which was probably best for anyone nearby. He had a scarred face that could quite possibly damage them for good if they got too close or stared too long.

He looked back at a group of goth kids a short distance away. They were sheltered by a broken awning, and they leaned against security bars that covered a store window. This was the perfect setting for Daniel—dismal weather; vulnerable kids unable to find proper protection. For anyone else it couldn't get any worse, but for Daniel it was like spring time blossoms.

He saw a bus pull to a stop in front of them. The kids paid no attention, but Daniel did. He moved from within his shadow. The kids were certainly intriguing for him, but he felt he had watched them long enough. They weren't doing anything to up his entertainment value. Maybe the bus would.

Daniel watched the rain drive against a dark window as if its existence was threatened by a menacing force. Naw, he thought. The kids definitely showed more promise. He began to look back when suddenly, a lightning bolt revealed a man in one of the windows staring straight at him.

Daniel took a step back into the darkness, but he could tell the man was deep in thought. He could be wearing a clown nose and big, floppy shoes, and the man still wouldn't notice him. Daniel continued watching. He was extremely handsome—cut straight out of a fashion magazine—but that was not what caught Daniel's attention.

It was the white priest's collar, highlighted by his black shirt, which literally buckled Daniel's knees. He turned away and wiped rain boiling on his face that dripped into tiny balls of flame.

CHAPTER 4

JADA WATCHED THE BUS PULL AWAY as she clung to her boyfriend Seth. She stood under part of the awning, but it wasn't doing much to keep her from getting soaked. There was something about being here that didn't sit right with her, but Seth wasn't going anywhere so neither was she. Being on the street left her vulnerable, so Seth had become her protection. Being anywhere else, and with anyone else, simply didn't make sense. It was better than where she had come from. Much better than the hand that had driven her away from that godforsaken home.

Seth had found her out here, and there was no reason not to want what he offered. She knew Seth was different, though. The clothes he wore; his hair, and his made up face. This place had been part of him since birth, literally. His mother had been a prostitute, and she had given birth to him next to another whore who just happened to be working at the time. From then on, he had been passed around until he became old enough to make some sense out of these streets. That story was what attracted Jada to him the most. Who better could she turn to for protection, she had always thought.

Replacing the bus was a low riding, fully customized, foreign car. No others, just one car approached Jada slowly, with rap music pounding. She knew the driver, but she couldn't see him through the tint. She also knew the storm was now her smallest problem.

Seth made a move and walked away. Jada stayed with him; so did the car. She didn't look up, and neither did Seth. Just avoid eye contact, she thought. She knew Seth was thinking the same thing, but the pulsating jukebox kept their pace.

Suddenly, the music stopped. The car stopped. Seth stopped. Why, Jada had no idea. This is when they should be running. She tried to keep him moving, but it was no use. The dark window powered down. Jada focused on Seth who looked straight ahead. He must have been thinking he had to face this at some point, she thought. *But now? Oh well, I guess it's as good a time as any.*

She turned slightly to see Louie Castellani—calm, cool, and dry. He looked annoyed and entertained at the same time—like he was watching a shitty street act, but he knew there was gonna be a screw up.

"The rain's got you lookin' like a weasel," he said.

"I don't have it. Ten grand. It's a lot," Seth replied.

"No, not a weasel. More like a rat." Louie shook his head.

"Get in the car."

"No, man, no! I need more time."

Seth quickly began to move away. Jada followed him. This time she had to keep him moving. They were younger and much more motivated to get as far away from this thug as possible.

"Just a few more days," Seth pleaded.

Again, Louie drove alongside them. Jada pushed Seth, trying to make a surge out of there. Seth was reluctant for some reason, though.

"You ever seen a wet rat up close? It'll look like it's tryin' to fuck with ya."

Jada cringed with the roar of the engine. She stopped and pulled Seth back as the car jumped onto the sidewalk. She breathed heavily and looked around frantically for another way out of this. The door swung open. Louie pounced on Seth, backing him into an empty parking lot with his hand securely around his neck.

"Just like you, you little, fuckin' shit!"

Seth could barely talk. "I'll get it. Just—"

"But a wet weasel will just slip through your fingers if you aren't constantly watching."

She watched his eyes penetrating Seth's. She saw his fingers digging deeper into Seth's neck.

"You can't be a rat and a weasel at the same time. Didn't you know that?"

Jada frantically tried to pull Louie off. "I know who's got—"

"So, which one's it gonna be? You gonna try to screw me or—"

Jada screamed, "You're gonna kill him!"

Louie pushed her away while he still held tightly on to Seth's neck.

Jada fell to the ground but recovered instantly. "It wasn't even for him. We just need to get to—" She quickly realized she was about to say too much. "We just need more—"

Louie turned to Seth. "You've got a partner now?" He looked back at Jada. "Get to who? You tellin' me this random isn't who I'm dealin' with?"

Again, Jada pulled on Louie's arm. "That's right. Someone else. I can help you."

Louie pushed her away but with less force this time. He took his hand off Seth's neck.

Jada was instantly relieved. She instinctively helped Seth as he fell to his knees while gasping for air. She hadn't planned to say what she did, but whatever, it seemed to be working. Now if she could only keep talking her way out of it.

She looked back to Louie who swiftly took a gun from the waist of his pants and held it to Seth's head. Her eyes popped without understanding how this could suddenly turn so terribly wrong.

Jada went for his arm again, but he stopped her. "I can get you stuff. Good stuff," she said. Jada went to his pants. "Or anything you want."

Louie held her back.

Jada quickly looked away as lightning flashed her eyes

immediately followed by a crack of thunder. She looked back. Seth buckled over with one bullet in his head.

Jada was silent in disbelief. She fell to her knees and stared at Seth lying lifeless on the wet pavement. She hysterically tried to get a reaction. She pulled his head up from the pavement, but Seth's blank gaze was all she saw. The asphalt beneath him started spinning. Running water sparkled against the black pavement as it turned red. She looked at her hand supporting the back of his head. It was covered in blood.

Louie intervened and held the gun to her. She didn't care about what he would do to her now. She just held on to Seth tightly, so Louie couldn't do more harm than he already did.

"Fifteen now. By Friday," Louie said. He moved away without concern for the death. "Never liked weasels much. Rats, well that's different," he said to himself.

Jada was left alone in the pouring rain, holding Seth in her arms. Blood ran through her fingers and onto Seth's face as she still tried in vain for a reaction. She looked up to the sky then all around her. She settled her eyes on the alley where she saw the shadow of a winged creature fading into it.

CHAPTER 5

MARCUS KNEW FROM THE FIRM HANDSHAKE and gentle smile that he had left a lasting impression with the man he'd just befriended. He watched him walk away as the bus they departed from left the terminal. He made his way through a door and was relieved that he wouldn't have to wait in the rain for his ride. Hopefully, that ride hadn't forgotten about him, he thought. With his brother—the way he remembered him—he could never be too sure.

Marcus walked by a young mother who sat, holding her sleeping child. She looked up emotionless, showing years far beyond her age. Her eyes begged for help, even from a stranger passing by her on a dark, rainy night. This was an immediate reminder of what he had come back here for. He continued to a window where he saw his reflection. His youth and a crucifix around his neck, completed his look of a newly ordained priest.

There was work to be done here in the neighborhood where he'd grown up. This had become his mission since his ordainment. He hadn't had anytime yet to see what the streets had transpired into, but he knew it wouldn't be good. He remembered the vacant, overgrown lots and the boarded up businesses; the crime; the drugs. He had been part of it all but never very deep. He had made sure he didn't dig himself into holes he couldn't get out of, but his involvement had been necessary to be sure he didn't stand out. He was young then; it was his only option, but as time went on, he knew he had to come up with another plan.

His brother was another situation all together. Ever since he had left—eight long years ago—he worried about him. He remembered his brother taking to the street as soon as he could stay out after dark. At fourteen, he had robbed his first convenience store. Marcus remembered being in the process of giving him shit for carrying a knife when just like that—completely out of the blue—he had busted through a door, waving the blade and screaming at a completely startled guy behind the counter. Marcus had been outside the whole time freaking out while trying to decide what to do. Then, his brother had fled into one of the vacant lots with bills flying from his hands. By the time Marcus had caught up with him, his brother had been backtracking for his fallen money. Marcus remembered how pissed he was that Marcus had overlooked the bills while chasing him down.

Soon after that, the knife became a gun; the money, much more. Marcus remembered trying to reason with him. When that didn't work, he tried to take the older brother approach—tell him what to do and what not to do. None of it worked, though. His brother was set in the street, and all Marcus could do was get away from it all.

That decision to leave had been tough for Marcus, and his decision to become a priest was even tougher. He hadn't been at the church for a long time, but as a child, he looked up to two people—his father and Father Burke of St. Paul's Catholic Church. He remembered the look on his mother's face when he told her he was going into priesthood. She was obviously proud, but concern for his brother and herself overpowered her expression. At that time in his life, he didn't feel responsible for his brother. He had thought of Louie as his demise which left Marcus no choice other than to do what he felt he was destined to do.

As time went on, Marcus had lost touch with his brother but not his mother. He knew his brother still lived with her, so he felt comfort in her being protected. Even though Marcus had no idea how deep his street activities were now, he knew Louie's heart was still with his mother. From that, Marcus thought he could take over from where he left off with Louie. Marcus knew he would have to come up with a different approach from years ago. He hadn't figured out what that would be, but it was certainly high on his list of things that had to be done. He was also concerned about another problem with his brother. The white collar around his neck would almost certainly get in the way.

With that thought, Marcus looked up to see his brother's

car pulling up to the curb. He shrugged and chuckled to himself. The low riding, fully customized, foreign car didn't surprise him much. Marcus exited the station. He adjusted his coat to hide the collar as he approached the car with a smile.

Louie got out and watched Marcus from the door. He was also smiling, kinda. "Must be a miracle from heaven above." Louie looked to the sky. "You appear, and the rain stops."

"God's miracles aren't intended to stop anything." Marcus stood at the car door.

Louie looked at him with a skeptical look. "I'll give you a lift but don't try any of that preaching shit on me."

"You above all that?"

"Above or below, it makes no difference. Just stay away if you feel like preachin'."

Marcus instinctively touched the crucifix lying on his chest. Louie was already in the car. Music started to pound, and the car revved—an invitation for Marcus to get in.

CHAPTER 6

MARCUS SAT A LITTLE APPREHENSIVELY at the kitchen table. Everything was just how he remembered it. His mother, Angelica, worked at the counter making breakfast. She opened the fridge door that was decorated with thought provoking comments, daily reminders, and pictures. Nothing had really changed except now the standout picture was of her hanging a crucifix around Marcus's neck.

It was from his ordination. He wondered if it had been there since then, or if she just put it there because he was home. He thought the latter because Louie would have taken it down, or more likely, ripped it down during an inevitable fight they would have had about Louie's activities.

Marcus had been so happy at his ordination. His smiling face in the picture was just how he remembered it. It represented the end of a long road with nothing but a positive future ahead.

He also remembered an empty feeling. His mother was there; Louie was not. He had been instantly disappointed when he saw his mother there alone. This was why he felt agitated now. Him being here could only be bad news for Louie. Without knowing what Louie was doing in the streets that Marcus left so long ago, he had a feeling it could turn out to be extremely bad news.

Marcus looked at a worn transit schedule he held but had lost interest in. "I have to get off where?"

Angelica left the counter and hovered over him while she took the schedule. This type of closeness would usually be uncomfortable for Marcus, but this was his mother. He had wondered if there would be some kind of awkward distance between them, but his mother didn't disappoint him. She hadn't changed at all. In fact, it was just as though he had never left.

"You're going to Clemonds and Andrews, so you need to get off at Birchmount," she said.

Marcus looked up at her, frustrated. "I'll have to let God lead me."

She pointed more specifically at the map. "It's easy, Marcus. Look, right here."

"You've been riding buses for how long? It's amazing you're able to put up with it," he said.

At the ordination she had looked different to Marcus. She wore a beautiful, floral dress that someone obviously had picked out for her. Her hair was done like he'd never seen it before. She even had makeup on and her nails done. Marcus had wondered if it was Louie's idea because she never would have done that on her own. *If it was his idea, why didn't he come?*

She walked back to the counter. "I had to put up with you didn't I, and look what that's got me."

The woman he looked at now was his mother as he'd always remembered her. Her hair was tied back, ready for work. It was greyer now, but she had the same look. By wearing no makeup, her face revealed soft features among some obvious aging. She had gained weight, but she was tall enough to distribute it well.

She looked over her shoulder, back at Marcus. She was proud of his priesthood and it showed. She seemed relieved to have him sitting here with her. It was a vast comparison to the disappointment she displayed when Louie walked into the room. She turned back to the counter. Marcus wanted to see her expression, but she hid it from him. Just from that alone, he knew it had been eight excruciating years for her.

"Anyone seen my keys? Christ, I'm gonna kill someone." Louie looked directly at Marcus. "Sorry, bro. You're gonna take some gettin' use to."

"Don't change because of me. God's prepared me for what you've got. This place isn't a monastery."

"That's where I should have sent your brother a long time ago," Angelica said.

Louie leaned in, close to Marcus. He whispered, "Let me know when you're ready for what I got, man. This shit's twice what you've seen."

Marcus turned away, pretending he didn't hear. He took a

deep breath. He started to say something, but looked back at the transit schedule instead. He'd figured Louie would try to pull him back into street life. He just didn't think he would be this fast and direct.

Angelica continued at the counter then turned to Louie. "At least offer your brother a ride. He's got to go halfway across town."

Louie was looking for his keys again. "Find my keys and—"

"No thanks. No rides. I've found my way this far."

"Where you goin'?" Louie asked.

"He's starting up St. Paul's again," Angelica proudly responded.

"Fuckin' right. Wish these bastards would stay in one place." He turned from the counter and pocketed his keys. "You said St. Paul's?"

Marcus noticed Angelica look away. He also noticed that Louie was amused, like he just caught on to a joke.

"Remember, twice the shit you've seen. Fuck, man, you're gonna need it," Louie said with a snicker. He took his iPhone from his pocket, tapped the screen, and started to leave. "Come on."

Marcus didn't move from the table. Louie didn't look back.

"What's your cell number?" Louie said from the front door.

"Don't mind him, Marcus. He's not worth the trouble," Angelica commented.

"Sounds like I'll have no choice." He gave a confronting look to Angelica. He knew something was up, and with the church no less. "I don't have a cell phone. Do you?" He figured he might as well change the subject since St. Paul's was next on his list of things to do. Whatever these two were hiding from him, he would surely find out soon enough.

"Well, Louie got me one a long time ago, but I never use it." Angelica found it immediately in a drawer. She handed it to Marcus. "You'll probably have more use for it."

Marcus took it. He looked at it like it would make him disappear or something. He started pushing buttons. "Do you know how it works?"

Angelica gave him a skeptical look. "There's a reason it's been sitting in the drawer." She turned back to what she knew best.

Marcus continued with the phone. He suddenly felt like a time traveler, or the sole survivor rescued from a deserted island. He figured this thing would take some getting used to.

CHAPTER 7

THE WALK THROUGH THE STREETS was nothing more than Marcus expected. It was busy enough. Businesses that weren't abandoned were open. People were here, but no one seemed to care. Although it appeared to Marcus that he was the only one moving, he knew that wasn't the case. But their movement had no purpose, so they looked like they were standing still. He wondered if they just hung around like this all day. At least he was going somewhere. It seemed to him that everyone else was already there.

He turned a corner and walked along a side street. Less people were here. In fact, after a few steps, there was no one. He felt he was missing out on something—like he was walking away from the great event everyone else waited for. But he knew if there was going to be any extravaganza, he would be the one doing it. He was fresh here. Before he had left, he just blended in. Now he was the new kid. The new priest actually, and he knew the spectacular show would have to come from him.

Marcus remembered these streets well from when he had been a kid—younger than his gang days; younger than when he had tried to straighten out Louie. He remembered this as the best time in his life. It had been with his father, and this was the street they walked down on their way to the church.

Looking back now on the time they spent together, Marcus realized it must have been natural for his father to have Marcus with him. He doubted that it had ever been forced on him. Angelica hadn't put extra pressure on him to bring Marcus along. She just wasn't like that. Their time as father and son had been genuine. He had felt it back then, and he knew it for sure now; but his father died just after his fourteenth birthday.

There was a certain mystery involving his father's death. At least for Marcus there was. His mother rarely talked about it, and when she did, there were no details. How it happened; where it happened; why... Nothing about the event was clear for Marcus. The only thing Marcus knew was that his father had taken his own life.

He'd thought about that often over the years and even more lately. It never made sense to Marcus that his father would just throw it all away. He knew the type of man his father had been. At least he thought he did. Whenever he started up this debate in his head, he always decided that he was simply too young to really know the man he thought he knew so well. He had often thought about finding out more to clear up his confusion, but he never went through with any actions. He just let the clouds settle in, and somehow, he figured he must have preferred it that way.

Louie was just a kid then, and he had never really understood that Marcus would be his father figure from that point on. Marcus thought that Louie saw the death as an open door, even at his tender age of ten. But Marcus had never looked at it like that. For Marcus, the death of his father was like losing a piece of himself.

Marcus remembered his father mainly from the work he had done at the church. He had always been there; always volunteering; always helping. In fact, Marcus wondered why he had spent so much time there. His mother had never questioned it, and back then, Marcus had never thought much about it either. All Marcus had ever wanted to know was when he could go with him. He didn't know what the attraction had been, but something drew him there. All he ever did there was read alone in the nave among empty church pews; mess around in the basement and outside in the back; watch his father working in the bell tower. But it had been that time at the church that directed him to where he was today. When his father died, everything changed. But the memories lingered, and they drove his decision to become a priest.

Marcus rounded another corner and there it was. He saw the bell tower standing proudly above nearby buildings. He began walking quickly, encouraged by the idea that he would now run the same church he had such fond memories of.

How could he be so lucky to have been plucked away from that dismal street life and now find himself within the grace of a beautiful 19th century church? But the excitement quickly began to fade. Every step closer gave him a clearer understanding of what Louie and his mother were hiding.

Marcus slowed his pace until he came to a stop on the sidewalk. The thrill he had been experiencing moments ago was now completely gone. He should have known, and he scolded himself for being so naive. After a moment of staring at it, he shook his head and looked away. It wasn't himself he was disappointed with anymore, it was everything else around here; everyone else...

The church was littered with obnoxious paint, and the walls were deteriorating—partially from age but mostly from vandalism. It had boarded up windows. The grounds were overgrown. Actually, it fit in perfectly with the whole neighborhood. It looked totally abandoned, but that wasn't supposed to be the case. This was his assignment; his church. He was supposed to run mass here; give communion and offer prayer. He would take confession, and set up social programs for those in need. The priest from when he was a kid was supposed to be here to greet him; help him; mentor him... From what he looked at, he figured something must be wrong. Something was definitely wrong, he thought. St. Paul's was a ruin, but surely Father Burke made a mistake when he told him this was his church. Reluctantly, he headed for the door thinking there was no way someone was actually here.

Inside was no different. Marcus walked slowly down the main aisle beside dusty pews and toward a cobwebbed altar. He looked up at the cathedral ceiling and stained glass. The nearly destroyed pipe organ completed the reality of his broken dream.

Suddenly, the quiet eeriness was broken when Father Burke opened a door from the back of the sanctuary. He looked startled when he saw Marcus standing in the aisle but instantly showed gratefulness.

"Marcus? Marcus, welcome—" Supported by a cane, he limped around the altar. "Welcome to St. Paul's." He motioned back with the pride of a father passing the keys of a piece of crap to his teenage son.

Father Burke's movements instantly reminded Marcus of the time he had spent here so many years ago. Father Burke was more hunched over now. He didn't use a cane back then. He was worn and weathered, but he brought back the same feeling; the same desire; the same memories… But this wasn't the first time Marcus had seen Father Burke since his childhood. Father Burke had helped him get into priesthood. He mentored him, he was at his ordination, and he had been the Bishop who recommended Marcus be assigned to St. Paul's.

Marcus was stunned and didn't move. "This is God's church? I hope I'm not this lost for words facing a congregation."

Father Burke appeared shocked. "Well, I admit, it needs some work—" He looked around. "But look at this place. It's a classic."

"A classic? I think our Father has declared it a ruin."

Father Burke carefully sat down in a nearby pew. "You didn't expect the choir to be singing in perfect pitch did you?"

"Maybe not, but I didn't expect to have to write the songs."

Father Burke sighed. "Being a priest is all about sacrifice, son. I thought you knew that?"

"Father, this isn't what—" Marcus moved around cautiously.

"I'm a Bishop now, Marcus. I've given up a lot compared to others to get that. You're a priest now. You know the meaning of sacrifice. I know you do. We share some of the same."

Marcus stopped at the end of the aisle. He continued looking around. He shook his head slowly at the destruction. This used to be such an inspiring building, he thought. Images of his childhood flashed in his head.

"Don't you think we need mass here at St. Paul's again, Marcus?"

Marcus was aware that Father Burke watched him, and he also knew he was concerned. He was pumping it up, obviously. But for Marcus it wasn't working. He turned back to Father Burke with a disappointed look he could do nothing to conceal.

"It's just a building, Marcus. You're young, enjoy it. The tough part will be getting people to come."

Marcus looked up, following the beams that supported the ceiling. He shook his head slowly. "It's hell up there."

"You could say that," Father Burke said quietly, but Marcus heard it. Father Burke continued louder, "It's only dust. We'll get scaffolding."

Marcus moved toward the altar. "No broken glass. Amazing," Marcus replied sarcastically.

"Even Satan has taste I guess," Father Burke responded.

Marcus stopped before the altar. He looked back at Father Burke.

Father Burke smiled. "Go ahead, see how it feels."

Marcus moved closer to the altar. "What about outside?"

"We'll hire someone. This old beauty is a structural tank. It just needs a good cleaning, really."

Father Burke moved slightly with the assistance of his cane. It slid against the pew. From the corner of his eye, Marcus noticed a piece fall away. He was at the altar and turned to face the nave.

"Looks better already," Father Burke said.

Marcus savored the moment. "Does the bell work?"

"I wouldn't pull the rope."

Marcus moved toward the organ. "How about this?" He got there and touched a key—nothing.

Father Burke asked, "Are you ready to play?"

"Don't know how." Marcus sat on the organ bench and a pipe blasted out a note with a burst of dust. He jumped and saw Father Burke do the same.

Father Burke laughed. "You'll have to learn. You know,

for the songs you write."

Marcus shook his head, smiled and continued to look around.

"Welcome to St. Paul's, Father Marcus."

CHAPTER 8

FATHER BURKE HAD BEEN RIGHT. St. Paul's really was a magnificent building. Marcus watched from a distance as a team of contractors worked to put up scaffolding. Surrounded by an array of metal bars and wood planks, he was amazed at the steady sight of the bell tower that rose above. The church was small in comparison to others that had been built when this was, but it had served this neighborhood well. He imagined how small the community must have been when it was originally put up. It would have been for a very sparse population, and those people probably cherished its existence, he thought.

He remembered watching people in the congregation when mass had been held. Some paid attention passionately—clenching on to their bible while anxiously awaiting every word Father Burke had to say. They knew the proceedings without exception. They knew what he would say by heart. They knew when to sit, when to stand, when to kneel, and when to pray. They smiled on cue and had the hand gestures on auto pilot—like a handshake between men, or a fist bump between bros. Others never appeared that committed. They had woken up early on Sunday morning to be here, and this must have seemed as good a time as any to catch up on that missing sleep.

Back then, Marcus had never thought any of this was strange. He remembered the feeling of community here; the feeling of family around those he watched. Everyone seemed happy despite their sometimes strange routines. They genuinely wanted to be here, and they kept coming back week after week. What he did find strange was that his family didn't take part. Sure he had been there, and his father too; but their presence had been for other reasons that Marcus had never really understood. His mother had come to mass occasionally, but he knew she preferred to stay away. He couldn't remember, even once, the four of them sitting in a pew and attending mass like all the others. Maybe she didn't feel it was necessary to formally show up at every scheduled event. Maybe she just preferred to practice her faith on her own. Maybe it was something else…

He shook his head to clear the daydream. Regardless of what happened when he was a kid, now he was here to start fresh. He moved closer to the scaffolding and realized that rebuilding the church was very similar to the rebuilding he was currently doing within himself. Soon the building would be complete, but his job would be more involved. *Don't you think we need mass here at St. Paul's again, Marcus?* The message from Father Burke was clear. He needed this church to keep his life moving down the path he'd chosen, and others around here needed it more. This neighborhood would crumble to the ground if he didn't step in and do something about it. This was his mission as a priest. This was his calling.

He approached the front door feeling extremely different than just a short while ago when he walked these cobble stones. Back then he only saw failure in this building. Now he saw his future again. As he grabbed the handle that was partially falling off, he realized, for the first time really, this was his church.

***

INSIDE, Marcus wrung a cloth out in a bucket of filthy water. He looked down from the beams of the cathedral ceiling to see scaffolding dominating the space below. He was alone and found the area eerily quiet, especially from this vantage point. But it was from up here that he felt a sense of belonging—as if what he had just gone through to become a priest made perfect sense. He could see everything he'd been working for below him. He knew the church would be restored to its original beauty. It would turn out just like he'd planned it with Father Burke; just like it had always been intended. He saw himself in that plan too. It had never been his intention, or anyone else's for that matter, to be left out there in those dreary streets. He felt privileged to be in this building; destined to belong here.

He knew, however, he had not always felt this way; and to be perfectly honest, he still had doubts. He figured every priest must feel the same thing. The sacrifices were hard to overcome, but as time had gone by in the seminary, his beliefs and goals outweighed what he knew he would miss out on. He thought about Father Burke. Even he had talked about the sacrifices. He'd spent his whole life as a priest. Marcus could only imagine the choices he'd been forced to make. They probably still burden him at his old age, he thought.

Marcus sat down and let his legs dangle high above the pews. He couldn't help but think about the sacrifice bothering him the most. He had hoped that time would dull its sharp edge, but it still cut as deep as it always had. It had been brought up again recently, during his six months as a deacon, but how could he turn his back on all he had become because of a thing like the vow of celibacy? Simple, he thought. He couldn't. It had bothered him then just like it did when he left his life on the streets. It bothered him now, and he thought it probably always would.

He thought about the time when street life was the only life he knew. There were plenty of opportunities sexually for Marcus back then. He was strikingly good looking and a hot commodity for his female street buddies to pursue. But he had never been confident enough for any close encounters like that, so he shied away—kept his distance from the aggressive ones who would have ripped him apart had he given them the chance.

He remembered delivering a package to someone described to him as *a new customer with tons of opportunity*. He figured it would just be a routine drop. He would hand it off to some dude at the opened door of a heavily tinted luxury ride. It wasn't. The driver was the only one in the car. There was no tint and no dude. She, asked very nicely for him to get in. He did. How could he refuse? He was probably carrying twenty five grand worth of who knows what. But when he sat beside this *new customer with tons of opportunity*, all he could think about was the look she gave him and what he would soon be required to deliver. For anyone else this would be the tip for a job well done, but he got nervous—real nervous, real quick; and the package he carried had nothing to do with it. Fortunately for Marcus, she caught on right away, and to his surprise, she dropped the look and turned the meeting back into a business deal.

He remembered thinking, on his way home that night, if he just gave in, it would be no big deal. He would have that problem conquered. It would probably make this job a whole lot more interesting too. But Marcus didn't do that. He couldn't do that. Even to this day, Marcus hadn't done that.

He looked around and his eyes stopped at the altar. He imagined himself conducting mass to a full congregation. He smiled thinking about messing with the order of the prayers just to keep the routine seekers on their toes. He hoped he could make the experience uplifting and keep the sleepers awake. His confidence had grown leaps and bounds over the years, but that was only because of his progression into priesthood. He felt ready to lead others into a better way of life. That would include helping people find themselves and eventually each other. He would help bond relationships into strong friendships and marriage. The prospect of baptizing their offspring into the church excited him the most.

But Marcus knew he would only help with all this. He would be the one they could turn to for direction. He would give them the opportunity to include the church in their family lives. His vow assured him, though, he would never need that guidance for himself.

***

WHILE thinking about where the days had gone, Marcus stood among the pews that were once damaged and falling apart. He thought about the many men who had spent hours working diligently on this wood. Now they were all repaired within a 19th century Catholic church, restored to its original beauty.

He remembered the kneeling bars all torn, deteriorated, and broken. He had wondered if they could ever work properly again. He bent over to place one into its upright position. It was the same wood that shocked him when he first came here, but it was refinished now and covered with new leather; and it worked perfectly. He wiped his hand on the covering as if to clean away dirt, but there was none. It, as well as the pew attached to it, were immaculate.

He walked along the row remembering all the work being done here just days ago. He found himself facing the elaborate votive candle rack. He marveled at its cleanliness with a new, unburnt appeal, and he saw the opportunity for prayer it represented. He knew his congregation would find comfort here when they had concerns about their past and future. He thought about his future... *Lord, guide me and continue in your efforts as my savior.* He took an unused match stick, struck it, and lit the center candle. He watched the flame flicker and struggle to start. It began to soar, but it quickly died to a blue flame. As the wick burnt closer to the wax, the flame took hold and orange fire rose with the health of life itself.

Marcus turned away and was instantly overpowered by the breathtaking beauty of the organ pipes that overlooked the sanctuary. He thought about the anonymous donation Father Burke received to restore it. Marcus didn't know who the money came from, and really he didn't care. Neither of them did. He remembered how happy Father Burke was when he told him the organ would remain instead of their initial thought that it would have to be torn down.

From looking at the metal tubes supported in wonderful wood work, Marcus walked along the side aisle taking time to look at each of the stained glass windows showing classic biblical references. There was a scene of death and resurrection; the birth of Jesus; Jesus surrounded by little children; The Holy Family—Adam, Eve, Cain, and Able. He stopped at an image of the Archangel Michael, rising up to battle Lucifer. He thought the artwork was exquisite—they all were—but somehow this one stuck out. It was just a picture, but to Marcus it told a story like no other. It seemed to him that Michael was much weaker than the creature he held down. How could the pureness of Michael defeat such evil, he thought?

He turned, now at the back of the church, and the whole church flooded his eyes with its restored beauty. He remembered standing in this exact spot the first time he'd come here as a priest. It had been a hopeless building to him back then. There was no future here, he had thought. But with his drive and determination to make it something real, he created what he was now witnessing. He focused on the sanctuary and beyond it, the altar.

***

BEAMS of light shone through the windows reminding Marcus of how beautiful it was outside. The reflection brightened what he was already so proud of. He stood up straight, with his hands caressing the altar as he watched the colored beams dance along the shiny pews. He straightened the already perfectly placed platter beside him that contained a gold plated chalice and two communion cups. He shifted the two ciborium's already filled with hosts, although he had no reason to. Beside the tray, he softly touched the censer and boat. He looked up to the empty nave and said softly, "The Lord be with you." Then he passionately crossed himself.

CHAPTER 9

EVEN THOUGH THE SUN HAD RISEN a little over an hour ago, it felt particularly odd for Grace to be hugging a cup of coffee at this time. Normally, she would be rolling into bed, marking the end of her day. But today was different, and last night especially. Actually, it had been Jada who was strange up to this point. Grace was worried, and she didn't feel she could take her eyes off Jada.

Grace hadn't slept, and she had spent the whole time trying to get Jada to tell her what was going on. Right now, it wasn't the lack of sleep that bothered her, it was the lack of anything meaningful coming out of Jada's mouth. Over the past few months, Grace had given Jada her undivided attention. She knew Jada needed someone now that she had no one. Grace saw that and stepped up to help the girl in need. But it was mostly a one sided effort. Jada had never really opened up to her, so Grace didn't really know what to expect; but she had gathered up bits and pieces about Jada's past, and she knew something was off now. She knew it had to do with Seth, but what was Jada thinking? Grace had no idea.

She had been the first one to Jada's side after that bastard, Louie Castellani, left the scene. The gun shot had startled her. She had cautiously made her way from her apartment, down the stairway, and out from the alley to the corner. She had seen Jada holding Seth, all alone in the empty parking lot. The image of the two of them had burnt deep into Grace's mind. The only thing she could think of back then was that Jada needed help, so Jada had been with her ever since.

Grace was exhausted, and the thought of all this didn't help. She sighed, took her last drink of coffee, and put the cup down. She looked to Jada beside her—slouched over, sitting on the curb, and staring at nothing in the gutter. She remembered the rain, and Jada's eyes smeared with makeup. Her hair had been matted to her face. Blood had covered her hands and was streaked on her cheeks, making her look as dead as Seth. Grace knew at the time that Jada's loss was great. Jada needed to be with Seth, but Grace had to get her out of there. Jada shouldn't have been there in the first place, and she certainly couldn't be there when the cops came. Not that it would have made much difference, Grace thought. They probably would have ignored her just like they did the unknown street kid who got gunned down in a parking lot. To them, it was just another day; just another street incident to tuck away.

After Grace was able to break Jada's grip from the only person she trusted on these godforsaken streets, Grace had taken Jada back to her place. Having her there didn't bother Grace much. Grace was older than those who hung out in the alley and around here. They all knew her, but none wanted to get very close. Jada was no different, but she had never left. That told Grace she wanted to talk, but she just wasn't ready.

Grace had been just like Jada a few years back—no family; no home; no money—nothing. She'd built herself up from life on the street. Even though her apartment was still in the center of all the grime, she saw herself as someone who could make a difference for someone else. Jada had come to be that person; but so far, Jada's guard was still up, and her mind was probably on Louie Castellani.

All Grace knew about the situation was that Jada was now on the hook for fifteen grand, but he'd never come after her for that. Jada had always seemed ready to go a few rounds with him. To Grace, however, his threat was real. She was prepared to have Jada stay with her until that menace was gone. Now Grace worried that Jada had a plan to make something happen—remove Louie Castellani from her mind; from her life; from these streets.

When Grace realized something was strange with Jada, she pressed her for answers. Jada wasn't giving any information, though. *Didn't she trust me? After all I've done for her, she doesn't trust me?* Grace looked around at the sunlight shining through the cracks of buildings. *Was she trying to protect me?* It was supposed to be Grace protecting her, but it looked like Jada was suddenly thinking that protection would get in the way.

Grace looked down at the gutter—the same place Jada was fixated on. There was a piece of litter—an advertisement or a postcard no one wanted. Grace bent over and picked it out of the dirt with the hope of getting at least some reaction. Jada only looked up. Just as Grace went to throw it away, she noticed its message: "*In the name of the Father, and of the Son, and of the Holy Spirit, Father Marcus Castellani welcomes you to the re-opening of St. Paul's Catholic Church.*" Grace knew there was a new priest at the church. That would surely become a problem soon, but now her focus was on Jada—wait a second, she thought. *Castellani. Father Marcus Castellani… What the*—.

She looked back to Jada who was no longer interested in the card. That problem with the church was suddenly looking like it would happen sooner than Grace had thought. Jada continued to stare straight ahead at what appeared to be a bum coming their way.

He was far off in the distance, but Grace knew who it was. During all the time Jada had been with Grace, Grace had not only protected her from Louie Castellani but also this guy. She knew him as Daniel, and he was the reason the streets were like they were. Grace remembered him from when she was on the street, and his legend went back far beyond that. As far as she knew, he had always been referred to as Daniel. The strange thing for Grace was that he hadn't changed much since her street life. Back then he looked like death itself, and he still did. In Grace's mind he should be dead. He was certainly old enough, then and now. But he continued to lurk, to dominate; to control.

The kids Grace had been with worshipped him, just like the kids on the street did now. They seemed to see their future in his messages. If there was one thing they all had in common, it was that they hated where they came from. He hated everything, so that must have been their answer. Seth had been in deep with him. In fact, it had probably been his idea to get Seth involved with Louie Castellani.

Even though the kids, and the business owners— even the cops to some degree—felt the need to worship this degenerate, Grace would never allow herself to follow. She was stronger than that. She believed in herself, not some Satanist preaching greed and hate, and everything else he had turned these streets into. Grace saw herself as some type of antagonist to him. Not physically, but she offered an alternative. She spoke of changes that would make this place better for everyone. If she could only get them to listen. If she could only get Jada to listen.

She always worried when he appeared, but for some reason he never challenged her. He must have thought she was necessary—a source of comparison in his secret ritual sessions. She had often thought about what he said regarding her. She knew, though, it would definitely be the opposite of the blabbering mess that came out of his mouth. So Grace continued living among them, hoping some would see it her way.

Louie Castellani was another who opposed his message, but Castellani was a lot different than Grace. She knew they both played by the same book against Daniel, but Castellani wasn't taking direction from anyone. He probably didn't even know the depth of Daniel's influence, Grace thought. He didn't seem smart enough for that. If they were each gang leaders, one would have killed the other by now, but there was no organized effort coming from Louie Castellani. He just saw the streets as his. Daniel saw, not only the streets, but everything else as his. Grace saw them both for what they were. A gangster; a Satanist; the future, unless she did something about it.

Jada had been one of the few who appeared to be listening to her. She never had an opinion of her own, but she did hear what Grace had to say. At least until now. Grace watched her and knew that Daniel was the reason for Jada's sudden change. She didn't know how he got into Jada's head, though. Her plans were probably too passive for Jada, she thought. It looked to Grace that Jada had gotten to the point where a firm stance was what she needed, and Daniel delivered.

Getting a reaction from most of the kids out here was never a problem for him. Jada was probably an extremely easy target actually. He would have known about Seth, and he probably drooled over that vulnerability.

Grace noticed he was getting closer. Jada was suddenly more alert than she'd been all night. Grace knew at that point, all her efforts would be lost if she didn't get her moving.

Grace dropped the card and nudged Jada when she got up. "Come on," she said. "My eyes can't take anymore of this. They need some sleep."

Jada didn't move. Grace looked back to see him closer. It was obvious that Jada was his target. Grace pulled on her arm. "Come on, girl. No good's going to come from what you're looking at."

Jada remained still—fixated on the figure approaching. Grace knew she had lost her chance, but she wasn't prepared to give up that easily. She stepped in front of Jada to block her from his view. He was right there now, but he didn't stop. An inverted cross hanging from a chain around his neck caught the morning sun. It flashed Grace's eyes. She turned away but only for a second. When she turned back he just passed them, touching Jada softly as he went by. He walked over the card now laying back in the gutter. It burst into a small flame as he continued to walk away.

Grace remained still. It was a weak effort to protect Jada but an effort just the same. She knew she had been defeated. She had felt it before. She watched him with a combination of fear and disgust—a small animal afraid of its predator. She suddenly realized why he'd never harmed her. A cause without challenge was not worth pursuing, but a challenge without force was just the way he wanted it.

Jada got up and followed him.

Grace threw her arms up. "Augh, Jada." She wanted to chase after her, but she knew better than that. "Where are you going?"

CHAPTER 10

DRESSED IN AN ALL SAINTS SILK CHASUBLE, Marcus pulled hard on a rope which perfectly worked the bell high above him. He marveled at the bell's massiveness, and the ease with which it rocked.

The first thing Marcus had to do when he started looking for contractors was to find someone who could work on the bell. The man he had eventually found was reluctant at first. The man thought it was a hopeless case, and the whole tower would have to come down. When Marcus mentioned his father and his love for working on the bell, the man completely changed. It turned out this man had known Marcus's father, and it became his honor from that point on to work on the bell.

With every pull, the clang thundered within the walls of the tower. Marcus saw its beautiful detail from the sun that illuminated it, but that light never made it down to where he was. He knew he would be helpless if one of the pulls brought it crashing down. Marcus didn't mind, though, because this is something he'd always wanted to do. He had been in this place many times when he was a kid, but he never dared touch the rope back then. He would just watch his father working on the bell. Just being in here would have sent his father on a rampage if he'd known. But Marcus never used to worry about that. When there had been work to do in the bell tower, Marcus's father thought, or knew, about nothing else.

So he had seen, and heard, the bell before; but this was the first time he was in control of it. As he pulled the rope to keep up the bell's rhythmic movement, he realized this was the first time he was in control of a lot of things—his life being what stood out the most. He knew there was still work to be done. Even after all he had put himself through getting to this moment, emptiness that needed to be solved still surrounded him.

There was Louie for one thing. At this point he was unsure about what Louie was up to, but if he was to go by Louie's activities before he left, he was sure things would only be worse by now. Just thinking about all the decay in the neighborhood that surrounded this church made him realize Louie was likely the result of it or a major contributor to it, probably both.

But Marcus was here to change that, and he knew he could. He couldn't possibly feel more empowered than he did right now. He knew he had a long road ahead, and the problems in his way were not about to stop him.

He pulled the rope hard, and the bell's clang was his reward. He pulled again. No one around here had heard that sound for many years. He wondered how many out there had stopped what they were doing at the sound of it. He wondered how many didn't even know what it was. Whatever their reaction, it was definitely making an impact—right here, right now. It was the sound of a warm welcome—a new beginning—an answer for many in need of exactly that.

***

MARCUS stood at the altar with pride and confidence. He felt comfortable enough here on his own, but something was missing. This moment just didn't quite add up to what he had thought it would be. He didn't really know how this would feel, and his nerves had gotten the best of him leading up to it. Being up here now was fine, but he actually wished the excitement was still there. He'd grown to realize, however, that things usually ended up exactly like this—anticipation being the best part of everything.

As he looked to the nave in front of him, he was okay with the fact that no organist played hymns; no altar boy or altar servers accompanied him. It was just him serving his first mass, and he was proud of what he had accomplished; but he had to admit to himself that he wanted more of a ceremony, and more of an audience to present it to. He felt he deserved that just for the effort alone. All in good time, he thought. The church bell will ring again.

He addressed a handful of people sitting in the pews. "When we look at ourselves, we often see an unforgiving past, a regrettable present, and an uncertain future."

He noticed the faces he talked to were older—much older. In fact, these would be the people who did nothing to stop the creation of this damned place they lived in now. He couldn't imagine how they just let it all slip between their fingers. People usually fight for what belongs to them. This neighborhood used to be theirs; this church used to be theirs, but something swept in here and took it all away. Marcus could see in their faces, all that was left behind was the pain from letting it go. He had to give them credit for at least coming back, though.

Marcus had seen more of this pain when he appealed to the people. He had told them things could be better here; that St. Paul's would soon be holding mass again, and that change was exactly what they needed. But this wasn't the audience he was hoping to attract. He remembered these people being the most attentive, but he wondered how far his message had gotten. How deep did it need to go to make a difference? Did anyone even hear it? Actually, he knew they did. He had delivered it to many personally. The real question was, where did they go; why weren't they here?

He continued, "Questions linger for which there seems no source for answers. This is what the church is for."

He did see Angelica here, but she was alone. Maybe him being the priest would set the past straight for her and give her back the church he knew she loved.

Whatever kept her away before was definitely not the same thing keeping Louie from coming now. *Why wouldn't Louie come? Was he so wrapped up in the street that he'd miss his brother's first mass? Or was his brother being a priest something he just couldn't—wouldn't deal with?*

In Marcus's mind, he was confused, but his words were clear. "This is a place for answers to all your questions." He opened his arms wide to the natural beauty of this classic cathedral. "I will be here to answer them." He stepped away from the podium. "You may have felt that God has been missing from this place, but he's here now." He looked to the back of the church then toward the confessional booths. "He will respond to your questions."

He couldn't see any sign of Louie. He knew it was wishful thinking that he would come. *But my first mass, Louie? And of all people, you need this.*

"God is here for you," he concluded.

He moved slowly back toward the altar. A feeling of disappointment overwhelmed his thoughts. *All the work I've done. All the drive and determination I've put into this exact moment…* But all he was really doing was preaching to the choir. These were the same people he remembered being here when he was a boy. They didn't need to hear his message. They had it memorized. They remembered the routine, and they still seemed to think this was nap time. He sighed without looking up. He retrieved a container then turned to face the congregation, welcoming them to communion.

As the congregation started to gather in front of Marcus, he noticed an old man and a young girl sitting in the back row. The girl's youth and innocence caught his attention. She was who he wanted here. He needed her type to spread his message into the streets. But as he addressed those before him with hosts and a short prayer, he noticed she wasn't getting up. He also noticed the look on her face. She seemed depressed. The man beside her didn't get up either, but his expression was much different. He was fidgety. He looked all around with curiosity and determination. He wasn't depressed, he was obsessed.

***

MARCUS exited from large, gothic doors holding the processional cross. He took a deep breath knowing his first mass was done. Maybe the next one would be better, he thought. He remembered Father Burke saying, *the tough part will be getting people to come.* But how long would that take? How much more would he have to do? There was one thing he knew without question. The idea of quitting was not going to enter into any of those plans. He placed the cross on its stand and turned to receive the congregation.

An old couple exited first and greeted Marcus as though he had always been here, and the church had never been closed. This didn't surprise him much. They probably just thought they'd missed a few services. Marcus felt good knowing he'd be here for all the Sundays they had left. He smiled at them as though they were the only ones he cared about, despite his feelings of despair.

Others followed in a short line. Everyone was anxious to meet him. They seemed to worship him which he felt uncomfortable with. He smiled and tried to return his gratification by receiving each of them as though they were his only parishioner.

He saw Angelica still in the church. She held an unlit match stick while she stood alone in front of the votive candle rack. When he focused back on his parishioners, it was the young girl and the old man who stood in front of him.

The old man smiled. He offered his hand. Marcus couldn't help notice many scars on his face. He thought of the suffering this man must have endured during his life. *Was he here to find relief?* He wasn't obsessed. He was overcome with hope from being in this great structure. *Hopefully, I can make a difference.*

"Daniel," the old man said.

The girl was expressionless, protected by Daniel's charisma. She looked shyly at Marcus while he exchanged greetings with Daniel. Marcus smiled at her, but she turned away quickly.

"We're waiting for a better day. Your presence offers hope," Daniel said while looking slightly at the girl.

Marcus replied to the girl. "Come by anytime." He smiled at Daniel. He thought she could be the start he was looking for. Obviously, she was affected from living in such a depressing place. She probably knew others who felt the same way. She was only one person, but he was excited because at least she was here. He knew he could work with her. He wanted to work with her.

Marcus blinked with renewed encouragement. When he opened his eyes, he thought he saw an inverted cross hanging from Daniel's neck. It froze Marcus. Daniel turned away. Instantly, Marcus thought of Satanism; host stealing; making sure parishioners consumed the host in front of him at communion. Marcus was suddenly confused but realized they had not attended communion. He shook his head as if to remove the thought. *It must have been something else…*

They moved away and Marcus watched Angelica walking through the doors. She would be the last for him to receive. She hugged him, but his mind was still on what he thought he saw. She stepped back with a tear on her cheek. "Only your father's will could make this happen for you."

Marcus heard her say that. He knew she was right with him, but he couldn't clear Daniel out of his head. He noticed him look back at the sound of her voice. Daniel's warm and caring eyes dropped into a piercing stare. His lips tightened with a snarling chill of evil. At least that's what Marcus thought he saw. *I must be losing it.* He shook it off. *Strange how old faces can look sometimes.*

He turned his attention back to Angelica. He wiped the tear from her face. "You're the best that ever happened to him, and he's thanking you." She hugged him again. *And hopefully I'm giving you back the church you love.*

"Do you think Louie would come if I play his type of

music?"

She looked away raising her eyebrows.

"Come on." Marcus led her down the hall. "Ever see how the bell works?"

She stopped, as if suddenly paralyzed with fear.

"Ma?"

She stood anchored to the spot, slowly, shaking her head.

CHAPTER 11

MARCUS CLIMBED UP THE LAST FEW RUNGS of an extension ladder that took him to the steepled roof beside the bell tower. He felt with the season change coming, he should clean up what was left behind by the contractors while he still had the chance. The issue of having to deal with loose material and branches bothered him considering the amount paid for the reconstruction, but the fact remained—this stuff was still here, so he would have to do it.

He knew he shouldn't be complaining about it, though. Getting a contractor around here who was qualified for the work had been next to impossible. After Father Burke had left it all up to Marcus, Louie put him in touch with a few *dudes* who he *highly* recommended. One was ready to start right away. When Marcus asked him how many were in his crew, he answered that it would be a *solo effort*. Marcus knew to keep looking. Others he approached laughed the offer off, all appearing to know something Marcus didn't. He had realized his search would have to spread farther into other communities. When he finally found a company, they were reluctant to take the job. They said it was all about travel time, but Marcus knew it was really because of the neighborhood they would have to travel through to get here. In the end they had signed on; but when they were done, they couldn't get away fast enough.

While still on the ladder, he took a minute to look around the neighborhood. He could see it much differently from this vantage point, but the results offered no encouragement. The decay was widespread and seemed to extend farther than he could see. The shining sun made little difference. The streets were grey, buildings were dark, and grass was dead where there was any. Basically, life was lifeless. Marcus felt frozen—powerless to make an impact on an environment so engrained in its own misery, and the heavy breeze that blew into Marcus's face only chilled him more.

He had thought about organizing a church opening event—maybe a bazar or possibly a barbecue before the weather changed. The idea was to extend a welcome hand before he recruited people for his revitalization plan. But looking over the homes that he would derive his guest list from, it hardly seemed worth the effort. These people would likely be looking for something, but working for free wouldn't be what they had in mind. If he did go through with an event, he thought the barbecue would be best. *If free burgers and pop gets people to buy cars, why wouldn't it get them to come to church?* At least with free food, they'd be more likely to show up. Getting them to come back... He wasn't sure how he would do that.

"You seem to have more faith in your benefit package than you do in God," Father Burke shouted. "Just because it's a church—"

Marcus looked down. "That's where you're wrong, Father," Marcus shouted back. "He's the only package I need."

"Well, you're the only priest I need. How about you let his heavenly power deal with the foliage."

"And, exactly, what power do you think he has that can handle this?" Marcus looked at the mess.

"Exactly?" Father Burke replied. "Exactly, the wind that's going to make you part of it."

Marcus stayed on the ladder and looked to the sky. It was nasty up there—no question about that; but he had taken the time to get this far, so getting at least something done seemed appropriate.

Some of the leaves blew into his face. He shut his eyes and shook his head clear of them. While blinking, he replied, "I see what you mean." He looked toward the eavestrough. *Surely, I can free some of it, so the wind can do its work.* "I'll just see if I can—"

He left the ladder and moved carefully toward a branch that was caught. He looked down to see construction material—remnants of the finished work were the only things below.

Still within distance of the ladder, he worked to free the branch. It was stuck, so he pulled harder. It still didn't budge. He repositioned himself and pulled again. There was some movement this time—some hope, so he pulled again.

It came free, but he lost his balance and his grip of the branch. His leg hit the ladder, knocking it into a tree. He scrambled to keep from sliding. There was no use. His only hope was to grab back on to the branch.

It stopped him at the edge, and he frantically reached for the ladder. It wasn't there. His legs dangled over the side. He looked down to see the construction material below. The branch was the only thing keeping him from a disastrous fall into it. He tried desperately to see something else to grab onto, but only roofing tiles were within sight.

Stopping short of panicking, he tried to get himself back securely on the roof. The tiles were slippery and the extra movement caused the branch to break, sending him closer to the edge. The branch caught on to something he couldn't see, saving him from the fall. He desperately held on and tried to grab the eavestrough. He took a quick look down then made another attempt. He knew he only had a second before the branch would give away again.

Suddenly, the ladder nudged against him. He instinctively clung to it and sighed with relief. Again, he looked down, and the girl from mass was looking up.

That shocked Marcus. He fully expected Father Burke to be there, but the girl was his savior this time. He immediately forgot about his near death experience. She came back. He'd told her, *come back anytime,* and here she was. He took a second to look at her and celebrate his small victory. He felt like his smile was too big. He began to climb down then stepped off the ladder. "I think I saw my life flash before my eyes."

"Good thing it wasn't me up there," she said.

Marcus paused while he looked at her again. He was closer—right beside her actually. She was dressed seductively in tight jeans and a jacket—a teenager making a statement that had already been said. He stepped away slightly and a little uncomfortably.

Marcus responded, "Not a good story?"

She looked away and said nothing.

He continued, "Why?"

Still, she said nothing.

"I'm Marcus."

She replied, "I thought you were a priest."

"I am."

"Then Father Marcus."

Marcus nodded with raised eyebrows having never been called that by someone this young. He felt like he was just like her. He came from the same place she did, but he knew she'd be expecting more from him than just being another friend. She was here for his help, and he absolutely had to give it to her. "I'm a new priest. It takes getting used to." He looked at her as though it made no difference. "I guess, if it makes you feel better."

"Not better, just right. Better's out of the question."

Marcus didn't say anything. He just stared at her which seemed to make her feel uncomfortable. This was a troubled girl, and she needed his guidance. It's what he offered. It's what he was here for as a priest. But she was the first person who ever seemed to want anything like that from him. For those first few seconds, he had no idea what to do.

But he knew he had to do something. At least he had to talk. "Well, then, we'll start with right. Hi, I'm Father Marcus."

She smiled slightly. "Jada."

He smiled back.

Pounding rap music began to accompany the awkwardness. Marcus used it as an excuse to turn away then realized his brother was stopped at the curb.

The music stopped as the car window powered down. Marcus moved toward him, frustrated. "Do I have to put up a quiet zone sign?"

"Take a look around, brother. No one cares." Louie smiled as though he knew something Marcus didn't. "Need a lift somewhere?"

Marcus was suddenly impressed. "Well, now that I'm here, not really."

Louie was looking beyond Marcus at the church. "It's looking good, bro. Ya done fine work here."

"I missed you the other day when we opened. I must have been too busy to notice where you were sitting." Marcus stared at him to let the sting of guilt sink in. Just forget about it, he thought. He came now. It's a start. "Come on, I'll show you around—show you both around." He turned back to Jada. "I doubt he'll do it on his own, but—" She was gone.

Marcus looked around, completely confused—like he was suddenly somewhere else. He turned back to Louie. "Did you see a girl standing here?"

Louie smiled sarcastically. "You wish."

Marcus ignored him and looked back for Jada.

"I was gonna ask you about that and this priest thing."

He didn't see her anywhere. *How did she slip away that fast? Why did she?* It wasn't like he ignored her or pushed her off at the sight of Louie. *Right?*

CHAPTER 12

MARCUS KNELT IN THE FIRST PEW before the altar. He stared aimlessly at the ground. He knew he should be praying—in fact he had been praying, but now he was deep in thought about where his life had taken him. He looked up in disbelief that all he saw before him was now under his control. Sure it was just a building, but he knew what he had been through to get here; and now that he had brought this old, tired building back to life, he was sure of the opportunities it could offer others. But his lingering problem still existed—the place was empty.

He looked around to be sure of that. He was suddenly concerned that if there was someone in the back, they would likely wonder why this priest was praying for so long. *It's not that strange. Priests are supposed to pray for what seems like forever.* He smiled at his own wisdom. Luckily, no one was there. But if there was, him being a priest would surely clear him of obsessive praying disorder, he thought.

Slightly relieved, he stayed where he was—kneeling and staring. He thought about the streets outside. He thought about what motivated that lifestyle; what drove people to act so far outside the law; what drew kids into it thinking things would be so much better that way. Was it easier? Was it more rewarding to succeed in something that's not allowed? Or was there simply no other choice? He had been there, so he felt he should know the answer; but he didn't.

He had always had a choice. Even as a kid, he knew he didn't need to be doing the things he did. He never cared about being better than anyone else. He had nothing to compare it to, which would have made being a drug courier—a mule—seem easier. But after his father died, he didn't care about anything else. He didn't care about school or what people thought of him. He didn't even care what his mother thought. Something drew Marcus to the street—these streets—and that's where he found the encouragement he had missed by losing his father. He had known the streets were a bad place to be, but he could survive in them. He wondered what they were like now, though. He was sure they were much worse than when he had wandered them.

He figured the reason for the destruction was because no one did anything about cleaning it up. Surely, there were others who had tried to make a difference, he thought. He did, to this church; but from what he could tell, he was the only one trying now. Maybe others like him had been silenced or even worse...

He remembered it being this way when he was a kid too. There had been cops, but he couldn't remember anyone getting busted. Not for drugs; not for violence; not for fraud, theft, or sex. He remembered drug raids and street takedowns; but when he really thought about it, the guys involved were back on the street the next day.

Back then, he never gave it a second thought. He'd figured all the tough guys around him were smarter than everyone else. In fact, he looked up to them for beating the system. They were his heroes. They protected him and gave him what he needed. They motivated him to perform his next run. Why wouldn't he see them as his savior, back then? He had wanted to be just like them, and one day he got his wish.

It had been during an early morning delivery. The guy he'd been working for was older, even older than his father would have been. He kept using lines like, *early bird gets the worm*, which bothered Marcus; but he was nice, and Marcus had always felt comfortable around him. What made him uncomfortable was the size of his packages. Most of what Marcus had dealt with were pocket size, but this guy never did economy deals. His business required duffle bags. If he had been still operating today, he'd have his kids using knapsacks which would blend in better. Back then duffle bags were more popular, so Marcus had found himself walking in the streets just after sunrise with a bag full of something bad. He didn't know what was in it. He never wanted to know. He chuckled to himself. *Guess that made it easier.*

Marcus had known his destination, and he knew the guy

he would be dropping off to. He had been through this routine before, and there was nothing unusual about it this time until a police cruiser pulled up beside him. Marcus had been given instructions about what to do in this exact situation, but none of that registered with him now that his fast life was about to crash. He remembered trying to ignore it, but the car was following his pace. When Marcus finally looked the cop's way, the message was clear—*stop walking*. Marcus did. Then the message was, *get in the car*. At that point, Marcus thought about running—just drop the bag and head for the alleys. But Marcus didn't. He got in the car with the bag.

When the door closed, he immediately felt strange because the cop knew who he was. He had known his father, and he remembered seeing both of them at the church. He talked about how good a man his father was, and how sorry he felt for Angelica. Marcus realized the cop wasn't even thinking about what he was carrying. This was simply a social call, but Marcus was too young to make that work in his favor. All the time the cop rambled on, Marcus became increasingly stressed about the bag sitting on his lap. He became fidgety and irritated, looking around nervously. The cop obviously noticed, and the conversation changed.

He started talking about Marcus being out there all by himself at that time. He seemed to notice Marcus's fixation on clinging to the bag. Marcus tried to think about what he had been told to do, but nothing was clear in his mind. The cop stopped talking. He looked hard at the bag. Marcus thought at that point he was done. Thoughts of juvie filled his head; his mother's disappointment; the example for Louie… Then the cop reached over.

Marcus knew he should resist, but he didn't. He didn't just hand the bag over either, but his lack of action looked like he did. That would never have sat well with his employer or his boys when they found out he'd lost their goods. If somehow he managed to walk away from this, he would have to deal with them. Even if he got busted, he'd probably be back on the street just like everyone else had, so essentially he was screwed.

But the cop didn't touch Marcus or the bag. Just the door handle. He pushed it open, and Marcus remembered him say; *keep your head up.*

When Marcus found himself alone on the sidewalk, sweat was streaming down his face. He was disorientated and blinded by the sun peeping over the buildings ahead of him. The only thing that had bothered him, however, was that he'd just experienced two old guys, at supposedly opposite ends of the law, who spoke exactly the same way. He knew it probably meant nothing, but to Marcus it opened his eyes to what these streets were really like.

Then another car pulled up. It was the dealer who, as it turned out, had been watching the whole time. Once in the car, Marcus was instantly the hero he had wanted to be. He was wet and trembling but a hero for shaking off the cop.

When Marcus woke up from his daydream, he looked around and realized he wasn't a drug dealing kid. He was a priest. He looked at the altar and all the majestic qualities of the place he'd created. He looked back.

Jada sat in a row behind him, across the aisle. She had a knapsack beside her.

Jada asked, "How often do you do that?

He was startled to see her again, but he tried not to show it. "Do what?" He suddenly realized he was still on his knees. "Oh—" He shuffled back to sit in the pew. "More now than a few days ago. Remember, the roof; the ladder?" She just stared at him. "How about you?" Marcus asked.

"Never. The last thing I need is to go around talking to myself."

"I keep God close when I'm feeling alone." He thought about that and her reaction to praying. He had never thought about it as talking to himself. To Marcus, praying was the only way he could interact with God. It was the same as talking to anyone or anything. He wondered if he could really make a difference for this girl. "Come here, we'll talk to ourselves, together."

She got up and adjusted her jean mini skirt and showed no embarrassment for the short, loose tank top she had on under an unbuttoned jean jacket.

Of course Marcus noticed. He pretended otherwise. She sat down beside him, but she didn't seem to be interested in praying.

Marcus was suddenly uncomfortable. "If I look the other way, are you going to disappear again?"

"Why would you look the other way?"

She waited for an answer, but Marcus didn't respond. She was right. *Why would I look the other way?*

"Besides, that will just make you have to pray more."

So you'd come back, right? He smiled and shook his head slightly. "The lifesaving event lost its thrill when you left, that's all." She smiled like she understood, but he knew she wasn't buying it. Actually, she was right. He did want her to come back.

"I wasn't looking for company. You know, three's a crowd. Were you going to thank me?"

"Yes, you saved my life." Marcus took her hand as a gesture of thanks. "Thanks, Jada. I'm extremely grateful."

She moved closer. "Happy to be here." She looked deep into his eyes.

He moved away slightly. His body tightened. All the anxiety returned from when this type of thing happened years ago. He had no idea why he couldn't deal with it, but now he didn't have to. "You realize I'm a priest, right?"

She looked at him seductively.

Marcus continued, "I'm here for you but not—"

She took his hand and put it between her legs.

Marcus jumped back. "Jesus Christ, Jada! Look around!"

"Should you be using his name like that?"

"Maybe not—definitely not, but that's not the problem here."

Her seductive look continued. In the past, when Marcus showed his nervousness in situations like this, the girl would back off. He knew he was nervous, and he knew it showed.

Jada was different than the others, though. She wasn't going anywhere.

"Jada, that's not the type of help you'll get when you come here." He sat back down facing her. He tried to calm himself. He needed to. He needed to get through to this girl and make a real difference for her. If this was a test, he needed to be at the top of the class. "You're a sweet, young girl who's having problems. At least I assume you are."

She looked away. He was relieved that assumption backed her off. He watched her suddenly change. She became subdued—withdrawn. She started to tremble. He instinctively wanted to hold her and keep her warm, but that was certainly out of the question. "Tell me about them, Jada. I just want to be someone you can trust—maybe the only one you can trust."

There was silence from her. That's not what Marcus expected. He thought she would start to cry and lay out some of her issues for him, but she didn't do that. She didn't say anything.

"Who was the man you came here with? Your father?"

Jada shrugged. She looked back at him. "He's just trying to help."

"But it's not working?"

Again, Jada offered nothing. *She'll talk. I know she will.*

"Help with what, Jada? It can't be like you're living on the street. You'd be dressed a lot warmer if that were the case." He hoped that would lighten the mood, but it didn't.

"I used to be on the street, when I was happy," Jada said.

"What could possibly make you more miserable than that?"

"I wasn't miserable then. It was where we wanted to be. Someone just decided to take it all away."

"Living on the street is no place to be happy, Jada. It's just a matter of time before anything good turns against you. I used to be out there too, and I know about the good times; the independence; the freedom. But I also know about what it takes from your soul." He stopped, thinking he'd just gone too deep. If he was going to win this girl over, preaching God almighty would definitely send her for the door. "Come on. I have something for you."

Marcus got up and waited for Jada to do the same. She hesitated but slowly exited the pew. He watched her moving away. The dress she wore was short—too short. She bent over and picked up her knapsack. *Way too short*. He gulped slightly and closed his eyes. He started walking up the aisle making sure she followed him.

***

MARCUS looked through some papers piled up in the corner of his office. "Just when you really want something." He continued, frustrated.

Jada replied, "Like some heat?"

Marcus turned to her. She was placing her knapsack on a chair then she leaned against the desk. He laughed slightly. "The leaves are falling, and it's an old building." He turned back to the stack of papers. "You have to dress for it." *And a little less provocative when you come to a church would be good.*

He was relieved that she seemed to have gotten over what bothered her before. He looked at her again, smiling, then he was embarrassed, like he'd just seen what he shouldn't have.

She was watching him, seductively again, with erect nipples showing through her shirt.

This was partially hidden by the jacket, but Marcus had no trouble seeing what she obviously intended for him to see. He looked away. *Damn it, man. Get a grip of yourself. She's cold. She's not trying to seduce the new priest in town.* "I'm sure they're right here, close enough to touch. I mean—"

He closed his eyes. The tightening in his body started again. When he opened them, she seemed to enjoy his nervousness. *She must think I'm a damn fool.*

"There they are." He knew he just needed to focus on what he came here for. He had his mind set on accomplishing something with her, so just get to it, he thought.

Avoiding eye contact, he passed in front of her, toward another pile of paper.

She stopped him with her leg.

He took a deep breath. He tried to control himself—control the situation—but he knew it was a losing battle.

"I see you feel the same way."

She softly touched the erection in his pants. With the other hand, she made him look at her—softly, gently. It calmed him down.

"This will help."

She took his hand and put it under her shirt.

"Me."

He didn't move. He didn't resist either. The sensation from what he touched tingled through his whole body. He watched her close her eyes. He knew she wanted him to take over, but he had no idea what to do. He wanted to stop what he was doing, but the feeling was like nothing he'd ever felt before. It wasn't just the touch of her breast, it was an overwhelming sense of passion that kept him from moving away.

For all those years, he had resisted this exact moment, and he had been able to. Whether it was right or wrong didn't make any difference to Marcus. For him, it was never right. He knew this wasn't right either—definitely not now—but for some reason his fear of being close to another person was suddenly gone.

Could it be because he was leading now? In all his other experiences he had been a follower. He followed his father. He followed the dealers. He followed Father Burke into priesthood and now here to St. Paul's. But she came to him for help, and he felt in control. He knew that control was given to him for a reason, and this definitely was not it.

He also knew he had to stop. He had to move away. He had to redeem himself by getting this moment back to all he had intended. He had had nothing but good in his mind. Only moments ago his intentions were to help a young girl who needed him. But now, he was only thinking of himself,

72

and he was convincing himself that he needed this. He knew Jada needed him for more than what this moment would give her, and it would be up to him to make something better happen for her.

He looked down as she lifted one side of her skirt. She wasn't wearing any panties.

CHAPTER 13

IN A SMALL ROOM, dimly lit with candles, Marcus knelt before Father Burke. He could barely see, and he thought that was probably best. That would mean Father Burke couldn't see his face which surely showed a deeply troubled man. Even if his expression was visible, Marcus was quite sure he would not know of his current dilemma. The last time he had seen him, the only problems Marcus had were because of the church. He knew Father Burke was extremely pleased with the progress there, so this session would likely be a pat on the back. Assuming, of course, Marcus didn't decide to use this confession to actually confess.

Father Burke presented the sign of the cross. "In the name of the Father, and of the Son, and of the Holy Spirit. Amen." He motioned for Marcus to begin.

Marcus hesitated. He looked down. "Bless me, Father, for I have sinned. It has been fourteen days since my last—" He said nothing else. He didn't want to say anything. All he really wanted to do was walk away right then and there.

"Marcus?"

Marcus looked up, extremely confused. He turned away. He couldn't bear a face to face confrontation despite the lighting being in his favor. "These are my sins." Again, he paused.

"I know you've had a troubled past, son, and with the death of your father. Maybe now's the time to relieve yourself of this burden," Father Burke said.

Marcus showed some reassurance. Father Burke appeared to have no idea, but Marcus felt like a convicted felon about to receive his sentence. *Only if I let that happen, though.* "Father…" He closed his eyes. "At times I have acted impatiently with the men we contracted to work on the church. I've thought negatively about many people within this neighborhood." He opened his eyes and looked directly at Father Burke. *I'll be forgiven. I know I will. It's the way it works…* "I have reservations about my decision to become a priest."

He watched Father Burke looking back at him as if he was waiting for more. He expected his expression to change; anger to erupt from him. After all Father Burke had done to get him here; to get him this church. *Now I kneel in front of him whining about wanting out.* If not anger, disappointment was sure to wash over his aged and shadowed face. It was that reaction that worried Marcus the most. It wasn't having to deal with starting over; not having to resist the urges that had taunted him before. It was losing the admiration from a man who has had so much faith in him. But the words came out of his mouth whether he truly believed it or not, and those words would likely burn a hole into the man he watched.

Maybe he did know more, Marcus suddenly thought. A chilling nerve rushed through his entire body. That realization made Marcus think it wouldn't just disappoint Father Burke, it would likely disgust him. The reality of it would be crushing, but Father Burke wasn't showing any of those emotions.

Maybe he was just waiting for Marcus to come out with it. Marcus knew he should be doing that. If there was anyone he should tell, it would be Father Burke.

If he didn't know, however, he was probably much better off. Marcus knew he couldn't get his head around saying the words that really needed to be said anyway.

He was relieved when Father Burke broke the silence.

"Can a mind this young be so clean?" Father Burke paused then he nodded.

Marcus was shocked by his reaction. He surely didn't know about Jada, and about Marcus not wanting to be a priest… It was like he hadn't even heard his admission.

"I told you before that others will react as though you speak in silence, but if you persist." He waited as if to be sure Marcus understood. "And, a man your age should see the robe as one with many colors." He smiled.

Marcus said nothing. He didn't expect Father Burke to be this understanding. He was certainly relieved, but he was conflicted with what to do next. He knew this was the time he should come out with all his sins. Father Burke's guard was down. He would likely ignore it just like he just had, but telling Father Burke of his weakness so soon in his priesthood... Father Burke was old and traditional in his beliefs. Surely, he would consider this sin against the vow of celibacy important, but maybe he would brush it off. *Ignore it, and it will go away?*

"You speak of no mortal sins, thus three Our Fathers and three Hail Marys shall suffice as penance for these venial sins," Father Burke continued.

"Father, what I just told you is because of—"

"Seriously, Marcus, do you think you're the only young priest who believes he's messed up?" He looked down at Marcus with a sympathetic smile. "There will be good days, and there will be bad. Same goes for brick layers, mechanics, con men, and prostitutes; even priests. If you truly decide you don't want to be a priest, it won't be because of words you say to me; and it certainly won't be moments after you've exposed to the world the new man you've become."

Marcus looked down as if to begin praying. He paused without knowing if he should say more. Father Burke was probably right. *Good days, and bad days. Priest, or not a priest...* He pressed his hands together. *If I leave it alone, I'll carry on and deal with this on my own. If I confess it, who knows what will happen.* He hesitated a moment longer. "Oh my God, I am truly sorry for having sinned, because you are infinitely good and sin displeases you. I am firmly resolved, with the help of your grace, never more to offend you, and I will carefully avoid the near occasions of sin."

He continued looking down. He knew it was Father Burke's turn now. His silence was deafening. He looked up to see Father Burke staring at him. Marcus said nothing more. A slight smile lightened Father Burke's face. He nodded.

"God the Father of Mercies, through the death and resurrection of his son, has reconciled the world to himself and sent the Holy Spirit among us for the forgiveness of sins. Through the ministry of the church, may God give you pardon and peace, and I absolve you from your sins in the name of the Father, and of the Son, and of the Holy Spirit. Amen," Father Burke said then crossed himself. "Give thanks to the Lord, for he is good."

Marcus did the same. He touched the crucifix hanging from his neck. "His mercy endures forever."

The look Father Burke gave him after that said it all. It wasn't just a look of knowledge, it was though he'd experienced deep sin like this himself. *He knows something. I don't know how, but he knows all about it...*

CHAPTER 14

MARCUS LAY IN BED, AWAKE. He held his crucifix, rubbing it slowly with his thumb, as a tear rolled down his face. He looked at the clock beside his bed—3:23. He hadn't slept, and he knew he wouldn't anytime soon. He couldn't believe that his all-encompassing decision to become a priest was now in jeopardy because of one, simple encounter. He really couldn't understand how he'd let it happen. Was he that weak, insecure—flakey?

He had never thought of himself that way before. In fact, he'd always been proud for choosing his own path. But that decision had been made based on his thoughts and beliefs alone. He'd never let any physical situations be part of the equation. He had thought long and hard, but the battle was only in his head—a war with no shots fired. In the end, he thought he had won, but now he realized he'd only beaten himself.

Jada represented the physical; emotional; sexual obstacle that should have been in play all along. Others could have easily played the same roll, but Marcus had always been a master of keeping to himself. For some reason, he finally let his guard down. Now, of all times… How could he possibly ignite this debate with the fuel of real passion? His youth was in the way as well as his attraction to girls. Now that he'd jumped the hurdle of confrontation, how could he possibly deal with this? This new argument blinded Marcus, and he seriously didn't know how he could let it fade away.

But if he did just forget about it, how wrong would that be? He'd made a decision to become a priest; something came along and challenged it. *Ignore it, and it will go away…* It wasn't like Jada would come running back demanding his unwavering love and devotion. This was probably just a joke for her or some kind of gang initiation. He would probably never see her again if he just carried on with his routine. But what if she did come back?

He turned abruptly to his side, uncomfortable in the bed sheets that had been giving him some emotional support. He cleared the sheets away and thrashed back the other way. Suddenly, he bolted up. *Christ, how could I be such an idiot?* He sat in the bed breathing heavily.

Marcus knew he had no choice but to see her again. He had to find out what Jada meant to him. He needed to know what he meant to her, if anything. The whole idea of him being a priest seemed trivial at this point. A priest with this conflict was of no use anyway, he thought. The only way he could let it go was to find her again and see if she was here to stay.

CHAPTER 15

THE SIDEWALKS WERE ALIVE with a certain kind of weirdness that only came out at night. He had decided to come here when it was dark so he could blend in better, hide if he had to, and slip away when the time came. He was prepared to discover what the streets were like now and determined to stay out here until he found Jada.

Marcus was alone but among young men trying hard to emit a sense of cool they could barely pull off. He watched women and girls, kids really, move in groups with their over made-up faces and strange hair. They wore what seemed like costumes to Marcus. It was an odd feeling since he'd been here, at this time of night, before; but it certainly didn't feel like he should be here now. He had left his collar at the church, so it was just self-consciousness that made him feel this way. Physically, he fit in fine.

He searched faces as he approached a bar. A group of

people came out obnoxiously laughing. They nearly ran him over. He considered going in, but he doubted Jada was old enough to be in there. Not that it would make any difference, he thought, but chances were he'd have more luck out here, so this is where he would stay for now.

He continued along the sidewalk. He looked down an alley beside the bar. A group of kids shared a joint. One kid saw him and informed the group of intruding eyes. They laughed and continued as though Marcus wasn't there. *Twice the shit you've seen*, he remembered Louie saying. He could only imagine...

Across the street was another group and another world to explore. He went there.

He saw goth kids loitering in front of a store with a broken awning. He passed them as though he didn't know they were there, but he was sure not to miss any of the made-up faces. None were Jada. He continued up the street and saw nothing but an empty parking lot.

Marcus turned back and looked at the goth kids who were now staring his way. He continued walking away and stopped at the entrance of an alley. He leaned against the wall. He looked back across the street. Suddenly, he heard a noise. He turned to look into the alley and saw a small figure watching him then disappear into the darkness.

A gust of wind rushed past him. It was cold on the back of his neck. Vapor, like someone's breath, rushed up and into his face. Marcus grabbed his neck and turned quickly. Nothing was there. He looked back into the alley. He started to go there then reconsidered. Something brushed against his side as if to urge him to keep moving.

This particular area felt extremely strange to Marcus. Everywhere else had its own oddity, but this alley was different. He felt a need to go down there, but he knew if something happened he would have no one to turn to and nowhere to go. Despite his reluctance, the desire grew rapidly.

Before that pull got the best of him, he did the opposite. He left.

CHAPTER 16

MARCUS SAT IN A SUBWAY CAR, watching aimlessly out the window at a dark tunnel whipping by. He had convinced himself that looking for Jada was obsessive, and no good would come of it. He had argued that she needed him, but he realized by looking for her he was only satisfying himself. She had forced him to ask new questions, but how would she provide him with answers to them? The argument went on all through the night until he had convinced himself that his place was at the church.

If Jada really needed him—if she really wanted him—she would come back. If she did, he had convinced himself that he would help her. He would find out what troubled her. He would help her become a better person. He would use that influence to help others be better people, and he would create a better neighborhood by doing so. He had found empowerment in this decision. He had decided that he would do it within the walls of St. Paul's, and it would be done dressed in the robe and collar that defined him as a priest.

There was a sudden burst of light as the car sped into a station. The conductor's voice crackled over the speaker, "Birchmount Street, this stop. Birchmount."

This was his stop. This is where he had to get off the subway and make that vision real. Marcus started to get up, but he hesitated. There just wasn't enough conviction inside him to make the plan happen with this doubt still within him. The doors shut, and the subway pulled away with Marcus still inside.

***

BACK in the same area he was in during the night, Marcus watched the alley from across the street. His encounter there left him troubled since he was sure he had seen someone. Could it have been Jada? More likely it was just someone waiting to jump him if he had stepped in farther. But not knowing kept him watching; waiting; hoping...

A familiar car approached, unmistakable because of its beat. He saw Louie drive by slowly, scanning the area. At first it appeared as though he was going to keep moving, but the car stopped farther down. The music stopped. Louie got out and crossed the street. He was busy on his cellphone, but he seemed to know where he was going. Marcus watched him walk through the parking lot.

Marcus began to cross the street, but before he reached

the other side, Jada emerged from the alley. She was carrying her knapsack. She quickly turned onto the sidewalk toward the parking lot.

Marcus continued cautiously to the other sidewalk. Their movements seemed strange to him. They both headed in the same direction, and they were both alone. He had no reason to suspect Louie in any wrongdoing, but they appeared focused on something. He continued his pursuit, now following the two of them.

Marcus easily saw Jada up ahead, but Louie was nowhere in sight. She had gone through the parking lot and now approached a corner. She looked into her knapsack, then continued walking out of Marcus's sight. Marcus never thought much about the knapsack at the church except that it reminded him of the duffle bag he'd carried for the old dealer. Maybe that was it. Louie was the dealer now who did huge deals, and Jada was his Marcus.

With Jada gone, Marcus hurried to the corner. The solution he'd just thought of was suddenly turned upside down when he heard noise from a struggle. Unless, this fight he heard was with someone else. He peeked around the corner and saw Jada less than fifty feet away, at a dead end. Sure enough, she was with Louie.

Marcus threw himself back against the wall—torn between keeping himself hidden and turning the corner. He didn't know why he was hiding, though. He'd come here looking for Jada, and she was right there. So what if Louie was there too. Probably Louie being here meant nothing good, so

Marcus would only be breaking up something that shouldn't be happening anyway. He was disturbed by the commotion, so he started to move away from the wall.

"Fuckin' bitch. If your life was worth what you owe me, I'd take it right now," he heard Louie say.

That stopped Marcus. He was confused again. He didn't know what they were arguing about, but he felt like he needed to. If he stepped around the corner, however, that information would certainly remain a secret regardless of their reaction to him being there. He looked around, anxiously waiting for more.

Across the street, he saw someone watching him. He seemed to have a problem with Marcus being a witness. His message was clear—there was about to be a price to pay for admission.

***

JADA struggled, but a knife against her throat had a calming effect. "I don't owe you shit." She had her hand in her knapsack.

"You inherited it. Now you're left with two choices. Get it from who you say has it, or bring him to me," Louie said.

She took her hand out, empty. "Go ahead, kill me. I don't give a shit. No one's payin' fifteen grand to keep me around."

"Sounds like you've already dug your own hole."

"Maybe, but I won't be using it because of your empty bag of wind."

He let her go, spun her around, and held the tip to her chin. It pierced slightly, causing a trickle of blood to run down her neck. She felt the sting but showed nothing to give this asshole any encouragement.

He snarled, "A bag that makes a lot of noise. Remember that?"

She looked away not being able to bear staring at Seth's murderer. She'd already blown her chance at revenge. He was bigger and stronger. She knew he was impulsive and hardcore. She suddenly worried that she wouldn't make it out of here alive even though seconds ago she didn't care. She shook her head to clear this rush of emotion. It was too much for her right now, so she simply had to get away from him.

"I have no idea why I've let this go on so long." He pulled her face back to force eye to eye contact. He squinted at her and shook his head with a chuckle. "Something I just can't explain."

She moved away without any resistance from Louie and threw the knapsack over her shoulder. She wiped the blood from her neck. She looked at the blood and began to walk away.

"Fifteen large. Next time, the bag bangs again," Louie shouted.

"Fuck you!"

"Choose your words carefully, sweetheart. Goth boy's advice, I'm sure."

She kept moving into an alley that continued from the

dead end. She didn't think she was in any danger now. If he was feeling impulsive, he'd have done it by now. She turned back to see if he was following her. He wasn't. All she saw was Louie folding up his knife and head off in the opposite direction, rounding the corner to the back street.

***

MARCUS was no longer pinned against the wall. Now he stood dead still in an inset doorway. The only thing he'd seen when he got the chance to look back was Louie heading straight toward him. He took a deep breath and held it as Louie quickly passed without seeing him.

The man from across the street lay at Marcus's feet.

After watching Louie leave, Marcus moved the man with his foot. The man moaned in agony.

Marcus looked around the corner, but Jada was gone. He ran along the dead end street to a narrow alley. He hoped desperately he hadn't lost her. Farther ahead, he saw Jada walking down a stairway. He was careful not to get too close; not to startle her in any way. After she was gone, he reluctantly made his way there.

Finding Jada was one thing. Following her was another. Outside was different, but now she was in a place Marcus didn't feel comfortable with. At this point, he thought he should just give up his pursuit. At least he'd seen her, and he knew where he should be able to find her again. His safety was at stake here, and going any farther would likely jeopardize it. It was just like the alley the night before. No one was there to help, and there was no way out. Then Marcus thought, *what about Jada's safety?*

CHAPTER 17

MARCUS FOUND HIMSELF in a damp hallway with a soaking wet floor and walls dripping with black, shimmering mildew. A rat scurried past him after its hiding spot was exposed.

Jada was up ahead, obviously unaware of him following her when she met a man. It was the man she was with at the church. He wasn't her father living in the suburbs and pursuing answers for his troubled child. He was a leader; a manipulator; a reason for this decayed place. Was that actually possible, Marcus thought? Could one man change the thinking of everyone, or was his threat so great that all the good people decided to hide? Marcus looked around at the underground cavity he seemed to occupy. *And to do it all from here?* He watched them quickly move around a corner.

Slowly, Marcus made his way to the corner, but they were no longer in sight. Instead he saw a teenage catastrophe of litter, personal trash, and Jada's knapsack laying on the floor. With that, Marcus knew this guy had the youth right where he wanted them. They would be the same kids Marcus needed. Jada had been one of them, and she was with him, so likely they all were. Marcus nodded slowly thinking how far out of reach his dream had suddenly become.

He noticed a closed door all the clutter surrounded. There was something on it, but he couldn't tell what it was. It was too dark, and he was too far away. He cautiously moved closer. It was a symbol. He shook his head, amazed; but he should have guessed. It was the Sigil of Baphomet.

Marcus stood shocked momentarily, but it made perfect sense. The neighborhood wasn't falling apart because of laziness and carelessness. It was the result of a satanic movement that had been in place for who knows how long. Marcus remembered nothing like this when he was part of these streets, but he was young then. No one would have protected him from it, but he had been simply too naive to notice or care.

Jada was obviously part of it, and the man was likely the leader, Marcus thought. He knew other adults would have to be involved in order for it to penetrate so deeply. He wondered if Louie was part of this; if Father Burke knew. It was suddenly obvious to Marcus that his position as a priest would be drastically different than how he had envisioned it.

He wasn't prepared for this type of threat, but he knew he had been put here to combat it. Whether that decision came from the wisdom of Father Burke or by the guidance of the

Lord himself, Marcus felt overwhelmed by the task at hand and frustrated that he had no say in it. But he had a church, and he knew there were people who wanted to be part of it. His perseverance could make that happen. He couldn't give up now. Everyone else already had, so he was their only chance.

He stood over the knapsack, unsure of whether he should open the door. Instead, he picked it up. He started to go through it. Suddenly, there were intruders from another direction.

He dropped it; they saw him. He turned to bolt out of here. After a few steps, he looked back to the knapsack. He lunged for it, picked it up, and fled.

CHAPTER 18

MARCUS SAT AT HIS DESK looking at the zipped up knapsack. He was quite sure it contained harmless stuff, but he couldn't help but imagine what he would have been carrying in a bag like that. If anything similar was in it, he would have another problem, but Marcus knew it wouldn't be left hanging around if that were the case.

He unzipped it and looked inside. He pulled out a gun. Continuing, he found something attached to the canvas. He fiddled with it and took out a small digital camera. He noticed it was lined up to a hole in the canvas.

The thought of what he'd just found sent his nerves raging. Marcus fumbled frantically through a drawer and found a USB cable. He connected it and left the camera sitting on his desk in front of a computer monitor.

After bringing up the camera's folder, he picked up the camera as video clips began playing on the computer monitor.

He watched a clip of a goth kid bent out on something while Jada provided immature commentary.

Next, a video of a group of teenagers at night in the street played. It was all gothic and obscure behavior—a satanic underworld.

Then he watched a scene of an old man preaching the word of Satan to a group of men and women—all adults; all professionals.

There was a scene of Louie getting out of his car.

And, Jada having sex with a priest... Marcus.

He dropped the camera and stared at its monitor. The video paused. His face, in lustful pleasure, was frozen on the screen.

CHAPTER 19

THROUGH SLITS OPENED just wide enough to make out the details, Marcus stared at the picture of himself receiving the crucifix from his mother which still decorated the fridge. The room had been silent, but now he heard glass clashing and liquid pouring. There was a crash then silence again. It felt strange to Marcus that such violent activity would disturb his peaceful environment. He didn't want any of that. He felt like he was done with conflict, or at least he had done all he could do to be cleansed of it. But now it was quiet again, and he was comfortable. Whatever had just happened was over quickly, and he was okay with that.

With only one eye, he could make out the surface sprawled out in front of him. It reminded him of a barren wasteland that would take days to cross if he was able to attempt it. His other eye was out of focus because it was too close to the table his head laid on. He was aware that he couldn't see properly, but he made no attempt to correct the situation. Not having to hold up the very thing that made life difficult was comforting and worth the cost of his visual problem. He was not able to comprehend, however, that his vision was only part of his impairment.

He noticed wet glass scattered on the floor beyond the table's edge. Marcus made no attempt to figure out how it got there. He had been holding a bottle—he remembered that—but his thought process was much too slow to place the bottle and the mess seamlessly together. A glass on the table came into focus, and he quickly realized that this was his last chance. He reached for the glass, lifted his head but only high enough, and long enough, to take another drink.

***

EVERY time Louie came to this place, it took him back to when he was a small kid. He had been brought here many times by his mother. Her intent was to have him spend time with Marcus, but Louie had never been too keen on letting his older brother watch over him. If there were other kids around when they arrived, Louie would quickly abandon Marcus and seek out some mischievous games that Marcus would have no doubt tried to put a stop to.

As the years went by, Angelica stopped bringing him here, but Louie never stopped coming. He had liked it here as a kid, and he could never see a reason to keep it from his expanding experiences. Slowly, over time, the park became less of a place for kids and more of a hangout spot; a drinking place; a hidden rendezvous for first time experiences of drugs, sex, and crime. All of these activities, in this exact park, had molded Louie into the man he was today.

He looked around and pieced together where the swing set used to be, but it was now a collection of deteriorating picnic tables surrounding a huge fire pit. The sand that was once confined within the walls of a kid's sandbox was now widely distributed which made the place seem desert like. Trees that once landscaped the area were stripped bare for firewood.

Even now, with Louie being in his twenties, he still came here often; but his activities were not as joyous as the ones he'd sought out when he was a kid. This was where Louie did business—his office as he often called it. He had single handedly transformed this piece of tax payer's land into a battle ground for drug deals, arms transactions, sex solicitation—any type of illegal activity that could possibly go down.

The reason Louie liked doing business here was because it had always been problem free for him. But he had a problem now, and that was Marcus. As he thought about how long it would take for Marcus to find out what this park had transformed into, he made eye contact with the guy he had come here to meet.

Louie's customer approached him, and Louie dug into his pocket and handed him a bag of blow. His customer inspected it; smelt it; tasted some then took a pinky nail sample. Louie took a quick snort to show his comradery. There were smiles from both of them then money changed hands. The deal was done—simple, no problem.

Louie turned away and left without a word being said thinking this was the type of game being played here now.

***

WITH the glass still propped up to his mouth, Marcus noticed it was empty. That caught his attention enough for him to sit up straight. He got a clear view of the broken glass. He wondered how that got there and immediately thought to clean it up, but his motor skills were having trouble keeping up. He rose slowly from the chair when a sudden rush filled his head. Within two steps he lost his balance, slid on the wet glass shards, and banged into the fridge. He stayed there thinking this was as good a place as any to think it out.

He began trying to determine what he would need to deal with the sharp, shiny objects surrounding the shoes on his feet. He found it hard to focus and quickly forgot about that. He opened his eyes wide, and suddenly, the reason for his current state took the spot light.

Jada... Video... Sex... Priest... Jada took a video of herself having sex with a priest? He shook his head being much too inebriated to put all of that together. Instead, he took on each thought separately.

Jada... The sweet, innocent, sexy, hot chick who was supposed to set the stage for all good things to come—*fuckin' bitch.*

Video… He couldn't believe it. A damn video was out there documenting his personal moment for anyone, and everyone, to see. Finally, this time had come, and of all people, someone like Jada got the nod to throw the first pitch—*fuckin' bitch.*

Sex… After all the years he had spent thinking about sex, he had decided it wasn't worth the trouble. Jada changed that in a flash—*fuckin' bitch.*

Priest… *I'm a priest for Christ's sake. Not a reverend, or pastor, or a minister; or any other name they've come up with to do what I'm supposed to be doing. I'm a Catholic Priest, and Catholic Priests aren't supposed to be having sex on tape with Jada—fuck-ing bitch.*

He pushed himself away from the fridge, slipped slightly on the glass again, and continued for the hallway.

***

FEELING a little lightheaded from the hit he took at the park, Louie counted his money and checked his inventory. He took another snort. What the fuck, he thought. The bag was already open. He looked at his cellphone lying on the passenger seat—*no messages.* He started the car, and with the immediate pounding of music, he was on his way.

This was going to be a business run for Louie. He had customers lined up and product ready, but he had only done one deal. He felt the coke working its magic, but he'd been like this often enough to know how to handle it. It was well within his limits for enjoyment, but the buzz he had on now would have to loosen up if he was going to make any money.

He shook his head and punched the gas to clear the haze. It didn't work, so chasing green lights seemed appropriate. What didn't seem appropriate was his brother. Not only did he have the park to find out about, but Louie also knew it was just a matter of time before everything else came out.

What's the difference anyway, he thought. Marcus probably already had a good idea what he did on these streets. He had done the same thing basically as a teenager. But did he know what was required for the job? Louie knew Marcus had done runs for guys like him. As a kid, however, he had probably been blind to what actually went on day to day. Louie's business required mandatory action sometimes, and there would always be someone trying to stop him. Many had already tried to change his well-being, but he wasn't prepared to let the new priest in town be one of them. Even if that priest was his brother.

***

MARCUS stood at the entrance of his bedroom. It seemed to him now that getting up had been a good idea. His vision was somewhat clearer, and his thinking ability showed some promise. He looked in his room but didn't enter. The bed was made, and nothing was lying around—a perfect example of the man he had been just a short time ago. He looked down the hall to another room—Louie's room. He hesitated then went there.

The contrast in hygiene and personal taste made it hard to believe they were related, much less brothers. *And look at the fine example he turned out to be for this neighborhood.* He exaggerated when opening his eyes wide and wrinkling his lips, just like anyone in his shape would. After considering what had happened in such a short time, it became even clearer to Marcus that his dream of changing things was exactly that—a dream. How long would it be before he got sucked into it all and right back where he started from? *Good thing I've got Louie to show me the ropes...*

Marcus pushed himself away from his leaning spot. He held his position for a few seconds before staggering toward Louie's dresser. He knew his balance was questionable, but at least he wasn't bouncing off anything. He stopped to look at a wire cage sitting on top of the dresser. Leaning in close, he tapped it lightly. Black fur twitched within wood shavings. That startled him slightly but intrigued him more. He tapped again, harder this time.

A rat looked up then suddenly bolted for safety with nowhere to go. It banged against the cage and smashed into the other side. It scurried along the back then flew straight at Marcus.

Marcus snapped back. "Whoa," he shouted.

The rat bolted for the wheel and ripped a path as though it was his turn to light the house.

Marcus shook his head. He watched the rat and felt a rush of adrenaline that sobered him more. He opened his eyes wide again, this time for clarity, then laughed slightly. "Dreamin' about Susie?" He watched a little longer then got back to what he came here for.

He went straight to a bottom dresser drawer but found nothing. He tried the next drawer up. He thought he knew Louie well enough. He knew why he was still living with his mother. Within seconds, he looked at bags of white stuff in both of his hands. He was right. Out there, this stuff was free for the picking. Stashing it here was as good as a safe.

He poured a small pile on top of the dresser with the speed and accuracy of a seasoned pro. No straws or rolled up bills were needed. Just one nostril, a finger closing the other, a quick sniff, and it was all gone.

He looked up to the ceiling then closed his eyes. He opened them a crack—just enough to enjoy the rat aerobics while a long lost, familiar haze began to set in. *Good thing I've got Louie...*

* * *

LOUIE walked up to a group that was partially blocking the sidewalk. He exchanged greetings with fist bumps and light hand slaps. With that and an active cell phone in every hand, he knew cool was not something learnt here, it was a prerequisite.

One of the guys immediately took a roll of bills from his pocket and handed it to Louie. He took it with a slight nod and another fist bump. He didn't bother counting. "The way it should be done," he said then slapped the guy beside him on the back of the head.

Just as another guy joined the group, Louie watched someone else start to leave.

"Whoa there, lightning," the new guy said.

The guy leaving stopped but didn't look at his confronter.

"Word's out the goth chick's packin' a fifteen K roll," the new guy said to Louie.

Louie looked at him curiously. "They always find a way," he replied. *Maybe for once, patience is about to pay off.* He looked around the group *But it's never good for business.*

The group began to break up as the new guy headed for the dude he called lightning. Louie left. He was relieved that no one seemed to second guess his lack of action against Jada, but he knew very well he'd let this go too long. To completely forget about it would be suicide out here, especially considering the level he was at. So hearing she had the money was a positive thing, but Louie wasn't stupid. If it sounded like a trap, it probably was. There was one thing he knew for sure, though. He was about to find out.

Well clear from the group, he took a deep breath and shook his head. Now he really regretted the two hits. He touched a building to steady himself. He knew about collecting debt well, and this was about to get real. A quick eye and snap decisions would be required, so he had to get his head clear and himself prepared. He checked his pockets. "Shit," he said to himself.

He crossed the street through moving traffic. His car was

up ahead.

***

A train screamed into the station, too close to where Marcus was standing. It rocked him back onto his heals, making it hard for him to hold his balance considering the shape he was in. Getting out of the house had done him good, but he was still intoxicated. The fact that he stumbled back, not right into the train, didn't mean much to him. He was still standing, however, and that was impressive, he thought. After both feet anchored him to the ground again, he stayed where he was while the train blew some more sobriety into him.

The windows flew bye like a quickly flipped deck of playing cards. The image of a man flashed. There was a pause. Possibly Marcus blinked. He wasn't sure. Suddenly, the man was back in animated slowness as the windows continued. *Louie was right. This shit's awesome.*

After the train sped away, Marcus noticed the man again. He was standing on the platform, exactly across from him. At first Marcus was disappointed because he realized the man was real, not something the coke had dreamed up for him. Then, the man's intensity bothered him a lot. His stare was piercing, and suddenly the terminal went silent—a deafening silence. Then came screeching.

Marcus couldn't stand the noise. He turned away and covered his ears, moaning with the irritation. He was the only one, though. He noticed others watching his performance.

They weren't reacting the way he did, but the noise continued until another train ground to a stop.

Doors opened right in front of him. Reluctantly, he staggered into the car. He clung to a pole as the doors quickly closed and the train started moving. He struggled with his balance, so he dropped himself into the closest seat. He grabbed his face with both hands and rubbed his eyes hard. Hopefully, he could wipe away what was left of his substance abuse. At his mother's house, the more he took in the better, he'd thought. Now that he was outside, he wished it would all go away. He knew it would, eventually, but when?

He slowly cleared his hands and opened his eyes, but the man was still there, burnt into the window across from him. Maybe it was the coke playing games with him, he thought. He took a deep breath. The man smiled with a welcoming grace of the nightmare he promised.

***

A goth kid stood in the entrance of an alley. He turned when he heard a noise from two others who appeared from the dark. He waited for another approaching them from the sidewalk.

***

A girl with black hair, black eyes, black lips—black everything—walked quickly with obvious motivation. She was being followed by two others she knew were there. Another joined her from a door that opened onto the sidewalk, but it did nothing to slow her pace.

***

GRACE stepped out from her apartment watching a large group that had formed in the alley below. Jada was in front of her. She stepped onto the balcony of the fire escape. Jada had spent hours preparing for this during which she said absolutely nothing. Grace had felt like an intruder in her own home. She wanted to shake out of Jada what she was holding back, but she knew she'd find out eventually. Grace watched her descend with the grace of royalty—Princess of the Freaks.

Grace had no clue what was about to happen. She was frustrated by that, but she had comfort in the fact that Jada came back to her. When she had left with Daniel, she thought Jada would be gone for good. But she reappeared late last night—hungry, dirty, and tired. Grace had hoped that she was done with the madman, but nothing much had changed. Jada still said very little throughout the day; definitely nothing that told Grace what she was thinking, and nothing at all now. But Grace knew she had come back for a reason which was probably no more than the sanity Grace had to offer.

Now things seemed to be amounting to something, though. Jada had a plan. Grace didn't know what it was, but she knew she just needed patience and let things happen. So now Grace watched, and Jada took each step slowly—a solo performance for the grungy crowd below.

***

LOUIE sat in his car waiting and watching. He hadn't been here long, but the evening had now turned dark which would be a much better environment for what he thought might go down. Louie knew that fifteen grand wouldn't have just dropped into Jada's hands. If she put the word out that it had, then it was more likely that someone was out to get him. Louie also knew he wasn't considered an angel out here and with what he had done to Jada's boyfriend... He shook his head to clear that thought while he considered what could possibly be in store for him.

Regardless of whether she had a plan to pay him cash or pay him back some other way, Louie couldn't afford to ignore it. His street cred was much too valuable considering the type of business he was in. This was a clear message for him to find her. He just needed a clear head which seemed to be in order now, a good vantage point—the parking lot was in full view, and a weapon... He had already checked his pockets—no knife, but he kept a gun in here...

He took the money, and bags of coke, from his pockets and put them in the glove box. He looked through carefully. No knife was fine, he thought. He needed more than that anyway. A panic suddenly rushed through him. He completely cleared out the glove box onto the passenger seat. He looked into the emptiness then slammed the door shut. "Shit," he muttered to himself.

He looked wild-eyed outside then focused on the parking lot. He checked back through the stuff on the passenger seat knowing well enough he wasn't going to find a gun. He calmed himself. If he played it cool, he'd be fine, he tried to convince himself. *She's just a kid. They're all just kids. Stupid, worthless, street kids.* Louie would be damned if he was going to let her, or them, control what she owed him, even without a weapon.

He looked out the window again. He hesitated, but he was determined. The best decision here would be to start the car and leave it for another day. He knew that, but it just wasn't sitting well with him. "Fuck it." He opened the door.

***

MARCUS sat by himself as the train entered a tunnel. The man he'd been imagining was there again. His reflection flashed in the window. When he looked at the seat up ahead where the man should be sitting, no one was there. Marcus's head seemed to be up to more madness. He really started regretting that hit of coke.

A voice from behind him whispered, "Jada's waiting."

Marcus turned quickly. No one was there. He turned back restlessly. *Shit. This has got to let go eventually.* Across the aisle, a man, who hadn't been sitting there a second ago, read a newspaper. Large print on the side facing Marcus read: "*Jada's waiting. Follow me.*"

Marcus felt a whole lot less intoxicated now. His head was clear. He was thinking straight, but all of what was happening made him feel like the alcohol and coke were still in full effect. He knew where he was, and he knew what he should be seeing. The reality of what he actually saw made it hard to believe otherwise.

The conductor's voice came over the speaker. "Birchmount Street, this stop. Birchmount."

Marcus got up. The man with the paper did also. Marcus saw clearly that it was the guy with Jada. His scarred face was something hard to forget. Daniel… His name was Daniel, he remembered. It wasn't an image or a reflection. It was undeniably him, but he ignored Marcus like a stranger would.

At first Marcus thought this was the same man he had been confused about, but this guy was ignoring him and definitely real. The image; the reflection; the voice were all taunting him, and likely just something running wild in his imagination.

They each took different doors. Marcus staggered with the movement of the train. *Maybe I am still hammered.* He staggered again because of the train's aggressiveness. He noticed Daniel standing as still as a tree.

The train stopped. The doors opened. Daniel didn't move. Neither did Marcus.

***

LOUIE leaned against a wall still waiting and still watching. It seemed odd to him that the streets were filling up with goth kids, but that wasn't his concern now. He was only looking for one, and there was no doubt in his mind she was among them. When he did find her, his plan would be simple. He would follow her until he felt comfortable enough to approach, considering he was unarmed. He doubted she would give him the same advantage, so he would have to act quickly. If she truly did have his fifteen grand, he would make the meeting short to say the least. If she didn't, her time had run out in Louie's mind. His actions would be bare handed and quick—quick enough for her weapon to stay where it was and anywhere but in her hand.

Taking Seth's life hadn't bothered him at all at first. It was simply the way things were done in these streets. But soon after, it started to sink in. It must be because of Marcus and the priest thing, he thought. He figured this was why he had given Jada so much time. He knew all along this didn't sit well with his image, but something in his mind let her take less priority. He knew, though, this time would come. Now that she was pushing the issue with street talk, it was time to put this whole thing behind him one way or another.

As far as Marcus goes, well having his brother as a priest would just have to be tucked away in his mind. This type of shit was bad for business, and for Louie, business came first.

***

MARCUS followed Daniel while the train left the station without them. From what Marcus could tell, Daniel didn't even know he was there. But the things that happened in the train had Marcus thinking. He couldn't get it out of his head that this was all the same man. He knew he should be on his way to the church where he intended to let his intoxication run its course. But something forced him here, and he knew he wouldn't be able to turn away even if he convinced himself to do just that. Even though Daniel made no acknowledgment of Marcus's presence now, it seemed to Marcus that he was attached to Daniel—like he was being dragged along with a rope.

Marcus kept his distance as they walked along the subway platform. Daniel headed for a tunnel. A sign overhead indicated it would take them to stairs and the street. Marcus started to get nervous. He imagined Daniel would turn and confront him there—in the tunnel, or on the stairs. If Daniel had this planned, Marcus would be helpless here on his own. But why would Daniel have anything *planned* for Marcus? Why would he have anything against the new priest? Obviously, he didn't, Marcus thought. But why did Marcus think he was doomed?

He considered stopping and heading back to the train. He looked back, but the train was gone. Either way, he would soon be alone down here for Daniel to do whatever he wanted. He turned back to the tunnel, and Daniel wasn't up ahead. That made Marcus's decision easier. It was no longer a question of what would he do. Now Marcus needed to know where he went.

He picked up his pace and entered the tunnel. Tiles on the wall identified: "*HADES STATION.*"

***

LOUIE hadn't moved. He watched the parking lot across the street. If she was out here, she would no doubt end up at the parking lot. They always did. If she wasn't already part of the living darkness, she soon would be. She lived among all the creepiness that surrounded Louie now, so he knew he would definitely see her. He didn't know if he would approach her, though. The longer Louie stayed out here, the more he felt like this was not about to turn out well, especially considering where he was.

Territory was something Louie knew very well around here. He enjoyed roaming rights through most areas, but the goth kids had a small piece. Right now, Louie was right in the middle of their space, and he didn't like being here. It wasn't that he was afraid or felt threatened by anyone. In fact, he had always made sure his appearances here left a lasting impression. This time, the numbers were against him, however, and he felt vulnerable despite his reputation.

He needed to get Jada alone. There couldn't be anyone with her or nearby. Judging by the activity building up, he thought this would turn out to be a lost opportunity. He figured he needed to stick it out, though. At this point he was unnoticed, and if he stayed right where he was, there was no reason that would change. He could see what he needed to see. He could decide what he wanted to do. When she showed up...

Suddenly, Jada appeared in the back of the lot, alone. *Just like I thought*...

All the thoughts about waiting to make the right decision suddenly slipped from Louie's mind. His score was right in front of him, and she should be carrying his cash. He was Louie Castellani. When he was called out, Louie Castellani answered back.

He walked calmly, but deliberately, toward the parking lot. He made no attempt to hide. He did nothing to keep all the dark eyes off him. He knew they were watching. He knew why they were all there. In Louie's mind, this moment was his. He was about to be paid.

***

MARCUS stepped onto the sidewalk from the subway exit. Having no confrontation in the tunnel, or in the stairway, was an extremely good thing for him. He definitely felt better being out from underground, but as soon as he got Daniel in sight, Daniel dashed into the street and quickly disappeared. It was like Daniel knew he'd been spotted, and now he had to get away.

Marcus was confused. He tried to follow, but he was forced back by impatient drivers. He rushed into the traffic, weaving in and out of cars to get across.

He plowed through a group of kids. He noticed the glare they gave him, but Marcus didn't give it any thought. He was too concerned about losing Daniel. He was preoccupied with why Daniel was now running from him.

Marcus frantically made his way along the sidewalk. He saw goth kids everywhere. He got to the parking lot and stopped. Finally, he realized he was within a group that reminded him of death. They were not concerned with him, though.

He looked to the main attraction. His obsession with Daniel was suddenly gone. He hadn't realized where he was until now. It was the same street he'd been on before. The same alley was just behind him. The same parking lot he had seen Jada and Louie in before was right in front of him.

Jada leaned against a wall, and a man walked toward her. He carried himself just like Louie did, but Marcus tried desperately to convince himself it wasn't him. She turned to see Marcus. Whoever it was approaching her, he could tell she was frightened of him, but she wasn't moving. He made a move toward her. Instantly, Daniel appeared.

"Sorry, Priest, this is a spectator sport," Daniel said.

Marcus realized all his suspicions about Daniel were right. There was nothing good about this guy, but he had to get to Jada. He continued, but Daniel blocked him from going any farther. He reached slowly for Marcus's crucifix. He touched it as if it may shock him.

"And you, a minor distraction to its grand finale, will be

dealt with soon enough. But for now, I don't want you to miss a thing."

Marcus knocked his arm away. "Play your games with someone—"

A kid pushed Marcus from the side. He turned to see many ready to pounce. He backed up and stumbled.

Daniel was again obnoxiously in front of him.

"Who do ya think's gonna win?"

Marcus saw the man getting closer to Jada. She still watched Marcus, obviously hoping he would help her. From a slightly different view, he realized the man was Louie.

Marcus made another move toward them, but he was blocked by the group. "You bastards! For Christ's sake—"

"That name again. What happened the last time you called him that way?"

Marcus turned back to Daniel. "What?"

"Did he save your soul or condemn it?"

"A damn set-up!" Marcus surged forward.

Daniel grabbed him with one hand by the neck and lifted him easily off the ground. Marcus gasped for air, paralyzed by the abnormally strong grip from this old, frail man.

"Priest, your devilish tongue around all these kids. Please." He turned Marcus to Louie.

Marcus struggled hopelessly.

Daniel yelled to Louie, "Look familiar, Gangsta?"

Louie turned. Marcus could see him, but his vision quickly blurred. He could tell Louie had stopped, shocked to see his brother threatened within an inch of his life.

"A condemnation I can guarantee," Daniel said to Marcus.

Marcus forced his eyes open to clear his vision. He saw Louie go for something from behind his back. He held up his hands, frustrated and holding nothing. Louie tried his pockets. Again, he held nothing. He looked around as though he was searching for some way out, then he surged at Daniel with a battle cry.

Marcus fell to the ground and gasped for air. He noticed goth kids all around him. He rushed up. He looked back where Jada had been standing, but she was gone. He frantically searched for her but ended up seeing Louie now being held in the air by his shoulder. Not by his shirt or any other piece of clothing, it was just one of Daniel's hands, gripped solidly to flesh and bone.

"You're nothin' to me, punk. Just like the old man that put you here," Daniel snarled at Louie.

Marcus surged. He was surrounded by kids, but he took two out quickly. He elbowed Daniel on the side of the head then tried to buckle his knee. All it did was make Daniel drop Louie. He turned to Marcus and ripped the crucifix from his neck. It began to smoke in his hand.

Marcus heard the sound of sirens fill the area. He saw the kids begin to scurry like exposed rats. He felt like he should be running too. It was instinctive. When cops came, you fled. No questions were ever asked. He saw Louie struggling on the ground with his shoulder. He looked up to see Daniel fixated on his crucifix. It was still smoking and seemed to be on fire in his hand. Daniel dropped it.

Two cruisers mounted the curb and squealed into the parking lot. Their headlights shone on Marcus with Louie beside him, but only them. Daniel was gone.

***

MARCUS quickly approached Louie's car from across the street. He looked back to be sure Louie was still with him. "Who is—," Marcus said. He headed for the passenger door.

Louie shook his head while he nursed his shoulder. He struggled to open his door. "Son of a bitch just screwed me outta fifteen grand."

Marcus dropped into the seat and pulled the door hard to shut it. He held on to the dashboard with both hands, breathing heavily and shaking his head. Whatever just happened was a whole lot more than Marcus had prepared himself for when he had left Angelica's house. Back there, he could barely walk, but now he couldn't believe how clear his perception was.

He knew Daniel was against him. He figured Jada was too, although, he could really see desperation in her eyes. *But that was because of Louie, wasn't it?* Marcus couldn't tell how Louie was involved in all of this.

Louie cut the music just after the car started. He pulled away aggressively.

"You really need to reconsider your career plan. Guidance from God—"

Louie gave him a quick look. "I save your ass, and ya just

gotta play priest. You must be short on happy churchgoers." He looked back to the road.

"My ass? I was fine. At least no one's tryin' to track me down."

Again, Louie looked over. "Won't be long, bro. The mess you're tryin' to clean up at that church is gonna take more than just soap and water."

Marcus looked back. "You're an expert on the church now?"

Louie shook his head, disgusted. "You sign on for Captain of Hell Chapel, and you have no idea."

Marcus didn't reply. Louie had hinted at this before, and he was right. There was something with the church. This whole neighborhood was against it.

He reached for his crucifix, but it was gone. He panicked, looking around with urgency.

He saw Louie turn away. The car accelerated.

CHAPTER 20

AFTER SURVIVING A CRAZY DAY YESTERDAY, Marcus stood at a mantel in his mother's living room wondering if he could make it through another or how many more like it he would have to endure. He had trouble piecing together all the events. How he ended up on the train was unclear. He remembered having an instant desire to be at the church, but he couldn't put together his steps from Angelica's house to the subway station and onto the train. From that point, however, he was pretty sure about what happened.

He hadn't thought much about Daniel since they had met at the church. It was Jada who came back, and she had been the opportunity he was looking for. To Marcus, Daniel was just another old guy. He remembered him with Jada in the underground hallway; the inverted cross he had thought he saw; the Sigil of Baphomet on the door... He knew those things should have sent him warnings, but he had been too focused on Jada. He was too concerned about what she needed from him and what she'd done to him.

He remembered Daniel's comment to Louie while he dangled delicately from his grip. *You're nothin' to me... Just like the old man that put you here...* He must have meant their father, but he had no idea how to connect this maniac to him. He wondered if Louie really knew anything about this. He certainly hadn't let on that he did, but he must be involved with Daniel in some way. Why else would there be an orchestrated effort against him?

He looked at pictures that were displayed like a collection of trophies. His father proudly posed with Angelica, Marcus as a young teenager, and Louie, a kid.

All Marcus really remembered about his father was his connection to the church. He was known throughout the community, though. Marcus knew that because people he'd met since his father had died respected him. He had known Father Burke well, but he couldn't think of any other significant people in his life. Of course Marcus was young then, and he could only remember what he had been exposed to. Who knows what went on in the dark corners of the gothic church? He thought hard to come up with a relationship between the two men, but he uncovered nothing. There must have been a reason his mother never went to the church... Which was probably the same reason his father went so much...

That thought was interrupted when Angelica walked into the room. Marcus looked up to acknowledge her. He took the picture he was looking at. She was smiling in it. He hadn't seen that look on her face for a long time. Maybe at his ordination, but other than that... "What was it like, Ma?" He looked at the picture. "The church, when Dad went there." He noticed her expression—a little shocked, but she tried to conceal it. "Why did he spend so much time there?"

"Why ask me? You were with him mostly," she responded as if she wasn't startled.

"Yeah, but I was so young. I don't remember him doing much there other than work. Why didn't you go?" He didn't know what to expect for an answer, but he could see the question didn't sit well with her. "Wasn't it a happy place? Were there dragons in the cellar?" Marcus looked up cunningly, with wide eyes and a smirk.

Angelica turned away and began to leave. "I don't have time for that, Marcus," she said. "What should I make for dinner?"

"Come on, Ma. Just pretend I'm one of the girls. Gimme some of that good Italian spettegolare." He put the picture down and chased after her.

"That's just it, gossip. All I've ever heard about St. Paul's is spettegolare," Angelica said from another room.

"So it does have a dark past." Marcus walked to the entrance of the kitchen. She was at the sink, but there was no work to be done.

"Everything and everyone lives within a shadow, if you listen to the gossip, Marcus."

"But the church shouldn't. People go there to relieve

themselves from that."

She turned to face him. "I said it was gossip, Marcus. Nothing but people trying to turn a good thing bad."

"If people were saying bad things about St. Paul's—if they're still saying things—don't you think I should know?"

"What good is it gonna do?"

"Ma, I'm the parish priest and trust me, there's no line up to get in."

Angelica leaned against the counter. She sighed, then moved back into the living room. Marcus followed her. Even though she was talking about gossip, he knew he had hit a nerve with her. He needed to know the hidden mysteries about the church. Louie seemed to know, in fact everyone around here knew something. Everyone except him.

She walked to the mantel and picked up a portrait of his father. She looked at him with admiration. Beside that picture, he stood in another with Father Burke. It wasn't odd for Marcus to see these pictures, but he knew they went deep with her. She could have easily put them away after all this time, but they were still there—a constant reminder of a concealed past.

"Constantine was so troubled before it all started," she said.

"It all started? What started, Ma?"

"Millennium Mayhem he called it, but he wouldn't say anything more." She turned to face Marcus. "Then, suddenly, he changed. Right away, in January of the year 2000. He was happier than I'd ever seen him." She put the picture back in

SINS OF A PRIEST

its place.

"2000? The computer date scare at the turn of the century? That's the gossip you're talking about?"

She stared out the front window. "That was just the beginning—the end according to Constantine. When everything turned out okay, he thought he'd won."

"Won what?"

"He didn't spend time at the church after that. He was happy but extremely different." She paused with that thought. "But it didn't last. Soon after, he died, and the gossip started."

This wasn't making any sense to Marcus. He didn't think it made any sense to her either. She was probably not comfortable talking about it because she could never explain it to herself. How could she possibly explain it to her son? He was the new priest of the exact church her troubled past originated from. He tried to speak to clear up his confusion, but she didn't let him.

"There was Father Lopez, profiting from illegal immigration. Then Father Honduras the pimp." She turned back to Marcus. "Don't forget Father Murphy—fraud, money laundering, payola."

Marcus was shocked. He sat down. The church collapsed because of corrupt priests. His father had died before all this happened. Marcus was working the streets...

"You want more, Marcus. There's more you know. It's all spettegolare, Marcus."

He didn't look at her. "Gossip to some, sure, but to others?" He thought about the names she'd just mentioned.

"Those are all the priests before they closed the doors of St. Paul's. It couldn't have been all gossip."

"It was all gossip, and it hurt so many. All because of one man."

He looked up at her. She was obviously set back by the memories. Memories that kept her away. Memories she preferred tucked away.

"Sii dannata, anima del diavolo! (Be damned, the soul of the devil!)" She walked to Marcus. "But now, St. Paul's has a new priest." She touched his face. "No more spettegolare." She closed her eyes while crossing herself.

Marcus went to touch his crucifix, but it wasn't there.

CHAPTER 21

DRESSED IN BLACK, Marcus looked ahead to the same stairway he had followed Jada to before. He checked the back of his pants to be sure the gun he took from her knapsack was firmly in place. He had done all he thought he could to prepare himself for this, but he was nervous and uncertain about what he was going to do next. Hours of trying to talk himself out of it only resulted in arguments for and against. In the end, his curiosity had won, so now he stood here ready for who knows what.

He'd been here before and that should have been enough information, but it wasn't. He was a Catholic priest. They were Satanists. He should be able to live among them and let them do their thing. They had their rights just like he did, but Marcus couldn't help think they had taken away everyone's freedom.

Among other things that concerned him, he had no idea

what would happen if his identity was discovered. Both Jada and Daniel knew who he was, and others probably did by now also. But his desire to know more drew him here. His determination to do something about what was going on would take him down the stairs. His passion for redeeming his sin would make him open the door.

***

NOW Marcus was in the same hallway, standing in front of the same door, as before. It was eerily quiet. He was surely alone because even his slightest movements left a crisp echo. He would no doubt hear intruders, but that meant his presence would be easily known too. He had to keep moving, but he had nowhere to go except beyond the door.

He touched the handle, and his hand melted into it as the door opened. He quickly pulled his hand away and stepped back. That had to be his imagination working overtime, he thought. As he second guessed this whole idea, the door continued to open. He could see inside, but it was barely visible. Its vastness captured his full attention.

Marcus stepped into black. In seconds, the room became visually disturbing—a satanic ballroom completely absent of anything Christian. He couldn't make out details, but he could see pillars that surrounded the room. Horrific gargoyles and horned skulls peered down from above them. Beyond that was unknown as the ceiling and walls appeared to be missing. The darkness that he was surrounded by left him feeling like a spotlight would suddenly expose his presence.

He turned back to the door. It was gone. He reached for it, but his hand disappeared in darkness. He pulled it back quickly fearing what might happen. This whole place had nothing but mystery attached to it. He wondered what it would be like if it was lit up like any other place. It must have been just a room, but something about it made him think otherwise.

He turned back and saw something beyond the pillars that defined the other side of the room. At first it was just movement within black, but soon it became clearer. A red garment appeared to be floating. At this point, he was convinced his presence was not secret. Someone was showing off their magic tricks or simply trying to scare the shit out of him.

As the garment moved closer, Jada appeared from within it. The garment flowed with her movement toward him, but when she stopped, the garment engulfed her like a slave clinging to its master. She beckoned him with her gentle sway, and again, the garment flowed freely from the subtle wind she created.

He had to admit to himself, it was all extremely impressive. She was impressive. He wondered how she knew he was here. If she knew, how many others did? He felt he had no choice but to follow her.

At first he was concerned about where he stepped because he couldn't see a floor, but that didn't last. After a few steps, he'd covered what looked like a great distance. He looked back to where he had started and shook his head in disbelief.

He found himself in another hallway as Jada began to move swiftly ahead. She was suddenly in a hurry, and she didn't look back. She knew he was following her, so her destination must have been somewhere she wanted him to be. He noticed others now. They watched him, but they made no movement toward him. None of this felt right to Marcus. He was supposed to be hiding, but there seemed to be no secrets in this darkness.

He entered a room—a chamber—where he saw Daniel, but Daniel didn't appear to see him. He was prepping a group of desperate, teenage worshippers. Was it Jada's plan for him to see Daniel in action? She must have figured he was Marcus's competition, and Marcus needed to see what he was up against.

"Remember, all of you, your only purpose here today is to greet, serve, obey, and praise the priests in attendance," Daniel said to the group.

Marcus remained unnoticed at the back of the room as Jada continued toward Daniel. She took a place beside him. She appeared to be more than just a worshipper. Marcus figured she had been just one of them, but for some reason she'd been promoted. Quite possibly that reason was because of what she'd done with Marcus.

"A meeting of this importance is Satan's wish. It must be conducted with perfection and without interruption," Daniel continued.

Marcus watched the worshippers kneeling as servants.

They clung to every word. They were all young, and they obviously wanted to be here. Marcus was fascinated, enviously lured into Daniel's world.

"Take passion from your worship of him, and you will be rewarded with eternal sin," Daniel said. "Sin is good, sin is power, sin is Satan," he concluded.

Then, without indication, Daniel was gone. Marcus stood shocked—mesmerized by the disappearing act. He looked all around for an explanation but saw nothing.

The worshippers held their positions. They weren't surprised by Daniel's sudden absence. They had obviously seen it before, and now they seemed fully prepared to wait until he reappeared. Marcus guessed they hadn't been dismissed, so they would stay there until they were.

Despite being startled, Marcus moved from the back of the room. He approached cautiously, but he was determined to interact. "His words represent greed, lust, and hate," he said. The group turned, as though Marcus was another leader they were supposed to obey. He energized with their willingness to listen. "God proposes honesty, loyalty, faithfulness—all things good when Satan celebrates the opposite. How can you expect to live with health and prosperity when hate and evil make up the very bed you sleep in?"

Jada moved toward him. She seemed encouraged and proud, but determined to grasp the center of attention. Maybe it was for his own good, he thought. She knew this crowd. She probably knew of Daniel's capabilities. Maybe she regretted leading him here.

A worshipper stood up. "Satan despises the word of God," he said then moved toward Marcus.

Marcus replied, "It's God's word that—"

"Who are you to preach his message here?"

Jada quickly stepped in front of the worshipper. "He's a priest testing your loyalty," she said.

"Yes, I am a priest but not—"

"Maybe it's your loyalty that needs testing," the worshipper said to Jada. He pushed her aside.

Another worshipper entered the room. He was bursting with anxiety. "Quickly, Daniel demands assistance for arriving priests," he commanded.

The group reacted instantly, including the challenging worshipper. At first Marcus envied their allegiance, but now it seemed cultish—something he wanted no part of. Marcus suspected, however, Daniel would expect nothing less.

Jada left with them also, and again, she beckoned Marcus.

Reluctantly, he followed. He knew he was digging himself deeper into this hellhole, but nothing could stop him now. There were people here—kids really, many of them just like Jada. They were vulnerable and brimming with questions. He knew he had the right answers, but Daniel had the upper hand. He was powerful and magnificent here. This was where he flourished, and he had these kids right where he wanted them. But Marcus could only see beyond that. He could only see these kids with him, listening to his words. As Marcus followed, careful not to lose sight of them, he knew they belonged in his church.

Marcus entered another room that clearly reeked of evil, hatred, and death. Daniel was dressed in a black robe. He stood in the middle of an encircled pentagram, tiled on the floor.

Marcus blended in among others while Jada assisted satanically decorated men and women to their seats not far away. He couldn't believe the people he watched now. They were adults—people who lived in this damaged community. He didn't recognize anyone specifically, but Marcus knew Daniel's influence had spread a whole lot further than just with the kids alone.

Marcus noticed the worshipper hadn't forgotten about him. Why should he? He had picked Marcus out as an intruder, and now he had the perfect opportunity to shine among his leaders. He watched Marcus carefully as he worked to usher in a priest.

A bell rang nine times. The meeting began with the unassisted lighting of black candles positioned at each point of the pentagram. Marcus cringed at the reality that he was about to witness a satanic ritual. Actually, like it or not he was part of it. He couldn't believe they really existed. He had heard about these in his faith studies, but he never took the topic seriously. He certainly didn't think he would ever participate in one.

Daniel crossed himself counterclockwise. "Hail, Satan. Lord of Darkness. King of Hell. Ruler of the Earth. God of this World."

The priests repeated in unison. "Hail, Satan. God of this World."

"Today we gather to spread the word of a new mission that will allow our satanic beliefs to continue controlling the world in which we live," Daniel said. He paused, examining his audience. "A new, Christian priest is practicing in the sacred church of St. Paul."

There was a hush among the audience. A fake hush Marcus assumed. He knew very well that his presence at St. Paul's was no secret. Marcus stepped back slightly, cautiously watching. He slipped behind a pillar then moved behind the seats to another pillar.

He wondered if Jada had known this meeting was about him. She'd set him up before. Was it possible she was going in for the kill? That didn't make sense to him, though. She didn't know he would come here. When she did find out, however, possibly she grasped at the opportunity.

Suddenly, the worshipper stepped out from the seats and interrupted. "I believe this man is with us here, now," he said to Daniel.

Marcus saw Daniel's immediate irritation. Daniel walked slowly to the worshipper. "Interruption angers me," he said quietly but loud enough to ensure everyone heard.

"But, Daniel, he was in the other room praising God and condemning Satan." He pointed to Jada. "And she protected him."

Daniel looked at her, then the audience. "Where is this man?"

The worshipper pointed to where Marcus had been standing. "Right there—" An empty seat was all that remained. He looked back to Jada.

Daniel held his composure. He motioned for Jada to come beside him.

Marcus watched her obey without hesitation. Was the worshipper right? Was she protecting him? He wanted her to resist Daniel. He would back her if she did, but he knew her head wasn't there yet. He also wanted to condemn her and what better way to do that than let the Satanist take over. But he couldn't. He had to protect her. He had to keep trying.

He watched her clinging to her own confidence. She moved toward him as the garment continued following her commanding movements.

"Is this true, Jada?"

"You'll allow this distraction—" She looked at the worshipper. "From a hopeless follower only capable of protecting his own motives?"

Marcus wasn't sure what Jada's intentions were. At least she wasn't selling him out. She was obviously closer to Daniel than any of these other kids, but it wasn't clear to Marcus if she truly worshipped him. She seemed to have some reason to protect Marcus.

Marcus could tell Daniel's patience was growing thin with all of this, though. He had an important audience to impress, and these kids were just an escalating distraction. Marcus watched him closely. His calmness seemed only skin deep. He needed to see his breaking point.

"My question, Jada," Daniel replied with his eyes squinted.

"Your doubt is with me instead of this loathing degenerate?" She approached Daniel, resorting to seduction. She caressed him with a school girl's passion. "A man of your stature should never waver facing such a challenge."

Daniel paused with a deadly look of reflection. "This is who I tasked with the goal of disgracing the priest. She performed exceptionally," Daniel said to the group. He smiled at her, but Marcus could see it was mixed with desperation. He touched her face. "But it appears she may have lost her faith in doing so." He turned away.

Marcus readied himself. This whole thing was suddenly turning against her. He could see Daniel was ready to snap.

Jada replied, "Whose faith is questioned when sin receives no praise?"

Daniel took a deep breath. Marcus thought that question would be his breaking point. It was obvious he was losing control, but he only reacted to the challenge with a look of annoyance.

Marcus admired Jada for not caving into Daniel's dominance. He was unsure, however, how long she could continue.

"So, do you know of his presence, here, Jada?" he said calmly.

The question was direct and needed to be answered. Marcus wasn't confident of Jada's ability to respond in his favor.

"He's—he's yours to be recruited," she replied.

Marcus could sense her nervousness. He could feel the tension, but she was right beside Daniel. She must have felt the steam coming off him. At first he thought it was just his imagination, but as Marcus focused in on him, he saw that Daniel was actually steaming. His head; his face; his eyes...

He watched Daniel turn sharply to her with a completely different look—the devil's pride.

"A Catholic priest is of no interest to Satan," he thundered. "Anyone who flourishes here would know that." Anger burnt his flaming eyes. "The faith that is represented by the garment you wear, can only be worn by the most committed worshippers." He ripped it from her leaving her naked among a circle of observers. "To lose your faith in Satan means losing all that you own—your dignity, your honor, your life."

Marcus knew he had to act. He stepped out from the darkness and stood prominently within the audience. He immediately saw Jada staring at him with pleading eyes—the same desperation she had in the parking lot.

Suddenly, what she had done meant nothing to him. She was helpless and doomed. He was her only hope. "If Satan intends to take all those things, including her life—" He held the gun and pointed it at Daniel. "I wonder how your celebration of death holds up among this group." He pointed the gun to the audience. "Open the doors that disappeared with my soul when I entered this chamber of hell, or a few more will be added to your sacrifice list."

Daniel stared back at him, then he looked throughout a

stunned group of observers.

Jada ran to Marcus and hid behind him. Daniel could have easily pulled her back, but he didn't. He let her go like he wasn't willing, or ready, to end anything now.

Marcus watched Daniel's hesitation. He held his position while Daniel walked slowly within the pentagram. This was do or die for Marcus. He was outnumbered. The only threat he had was the gun, and that could easily be turned against him. But it didn't seem like Daniel was willing to risk his valued guests.

Marcus watched him nod his head slowly. He looked toward the worshipper who started all of this and now seemed extremely eager to end it. Mysteriously, the doors around the room appeared.

CHAPTER 22

MARCUS FOLLOWED JADA, running wildly in an underground tunnel. Suddenly she stopped. She looked confused by where she was. She turned to Marcus, and her eyes popped.

The last thing Marcus saw before the haze set in, was Jada's mouth opening. Her expression told him of an imminent threat, but he just watched her. He waited for the warning. The look on her face was of her screaming, but the sound never came. What did come was a blow to his head that left him motionless.

He was still conscious, and he remained standing but barely. He felt the weakness in his legs. Details of his surroundings blurred. He could see enough, though, to notice the worshipper plow into him and take him down like a hungry boar.

At first, Marcus thought of fighting back. His mind threw

punches, but not his arms. He tried to squirm away without the help of his legs. Marcus knew he was trying to counter attack, but his body had not caught up yet. Meanwhile, he took blow after blow from the worshipper. He felt his head being lifted up from the ground. He saw the worshipper's face coming closer, then his forehead smashed into Marcus's.

That sent a shock wave through Marcus's body but kick started it. He turned away successfully. He blocked punches. He worked to get one arm behind his back.

Suddenly, a shot rang out. A single shot that echoed within the confined space. The punches stopped.

Marcus saw the worshipper look to Jada, then to him. He looked away, then collapsed.

Marcus lay on the ground. There was no movement from anyone or anything. The physical threat was gone, although his ears rang from the gun blast. His head started to pound. Adrenaline energized his body but only for a second. He calmed down knowing he had nothing to defend against. He stared at the life he had just taken. He was stunned, motionless—a murderer.

Now, he had no idea of his surroundings, or how much time was passing. He didn't think about what he had done or what he should be doing next. He only thought about the body; the lifelessness of it; the dead look on the worshipper's face.

He immediately thought about his father and the pictures of him. He realized he had never seen his dead body. His mother must have protected him from that, but he had always felt cheated by not being able to say goodbye to the man he loved so much. It was easy for him to imagine his father laying in front of him. He wanted to reach out and touch his cheek. He imagined holding his hand and placing it neatly across his stomach. He remembered the funeral, the hurt in his mother's eyes, and the casket being lowered into the ground.

When he focused back on the body, it wasn't the worshipper or his father. It was Louie. This body was so much like his brother—full of life and stopped dead in an instant. Since it hadn't happened to Louie already, Marcus thought his time would come soon. To Marcus, this image of Louie looked peaceful, though. It seemed that he was too far gone for anything but death to bring him back to reality.

Then, the face Marcus saw was his own. He was literally dead, right in front of himself. He wondered how it was possible that he hadn't died. His actions as a kid should have gotten him killed. His naivety should have done him in a long time ago. His confusion about what he should be doing... This would typically be the death of anyone.

But he was alive, and that must have been for a reason. He realized that he was just standing there now, staring at the body. All his thoughts were suddenly gone. Only the vision of death remained—this death; this kid; this sin.

Then he felt Jada pushing on him to get him moving. He got up but continued staring at the worshipper.

"Come on," Jada pleaded.

He looked at her. He knew he had to listen to her.

"Holy shit, man. Don't just stand there."

He still didn't move.

"Father, Father Marcus!"

He snapped out of it and realized he was still holding the gun. He let it slide out of his hand. It hit the ground with a stinging thud. He watched it settle beside the worshipper's head. Instead of picking it back up, he started running.

CHAPTER 23

WITH JADA IN FRONT OF HIM, Marcus burst out a door and into an alley. That was when Jada collapsed. He looked around to see where he was, but he had no clue. He was confused about what to do. A dead body, which he was responsible for, was not far away; now another body laid at his feet.

He thought about running, but he went to help her instead. Realizing she was naked, he looked around desperately for something to cover her with. He ripped off his jacket and laid it over her. She remained motionless, but he knew she was alive.

Marcus suddenly heard metal clanging close by. He turned to see someone running down a fire escape farther down the alley. He'd been seen. He hoped they were running away from what looked like a mugging or... Jada was naked. *Surely, they weren't running away from this.* He instinctively defended and started to lift Jada up to get away from this intruder.

He was too slow, though. She was there and feeling Jada's head before he could move her. The woman looked into her eyes, trying to get a reaction. Marcus laid Jada back down as he realized she was there to help. She didn't even appear to think Marcus was the aggressor. She must have known something. She knew who Jada was, but what else?

"Quick, help me get her up the stairs," the woman said.

***

JADA moaned as Marcus entered the woman's apartment with Jada in his arms. He moved her to the couch. He looked around, and what he saw wasn't much. This was just a shell of a place to live, but at least it wasn't the street, he thought.

"What happened?" the woman said. She completely took over caring for Jada while Marcus watched.

What happened? That was a question Marcus hadn't even asked himself. He hadn't had a chance to even consider it. He had thought he was in control; his beliefs would prevail, but he should have realized he was in over his head. Things were happening in there that didn't normally. Whether they were tricks or something else, he should have stayed quiet. But if he had done that, what would have happened to Jada?

He looked at Jada and wondered why she meant so much to him. Why was he protecting her? Why did it matter what that lunatic was capable of doing to her?

"Someone was going to die. I swear, it was kill or be

killed," he replied.

She looked up at him. "I mean, why is she—"

He looked away, frustrated about the secret he had just exposed. "Don't know. She was fine until we got outside."

"You're the priest, right? I'm Grace."

Marcus hesitated. "You know about—" He paused. *Christ, man. Don't give up that too.* "Who are those people—that psycho?" He rubbed his head and cringed when he touched the result of what nearly leveled him.

She stopped then continued to the adjoining kitchen.

"He's a devil worshipper, a Satanist," Marcus continued, answering his own question.

She came back, straight to Jada. "His fire burns much hotter than that." She continued with Jada. "We can't stay here."

CHAPTER 24

JADA FOUND HERSELF DISORIENTED in a dark, narrow passage. She had woken in an unfamiliar place, but she knew exactly where she was. She'd been here before, just not in this section. Actually, she didn't even know this existed, but it was unmistakably familiar. Its age being a dead giveaway. She didn't realize this place had so much to discover, not that she had given it any thought since her last visit.

She was dressed in an oversized t-shirt and barefoot. Mist showed from every breath, but she didn't notice the cold. She took a few more steps then wondered if she should just go back to where she had been sleeping. The mystery of this place kept her interest, however, so she moved forward hoping this path would lead to somewhere interesting.

She stopped when she noticed a door that was hard to distinguish from the stone wall. She had almost passed right by since the darkness hid it so well. She pushed it, expecting it to be locked or jammed. It swung open easily with an eerie creak that shattered the silence. She thought about how that alone would have sent the girls she had gone to school with into a screaming frenzy, but Jada wasn't like that. Especially now that she was on her own, Jada was pretty much up for anything.

She stepped cautiously into a small room with rounded walls. She had no idea what this could be used for until she looked up the wall of stone to an old, steel bell glowing in the moonlight. Its overpowering dominance left her with a feeling of helplessness if it ever came crashing down. She stared at the opening knowing it could easily smother her whole. The chime alone was big enough to smash her head wide open leaving her unidentifiable. Despite its undisputed supremacy, the vision of it from this vantage point was mesmerizing.

She thought about what that bell represented, and why it meant anything to her at all. It hadn't for an extremely long time, but she remembered hearing one ringing far off in the distance when she had been a kid. It had only been the chime of the bell she heard back then. She had never once gotten close enough to see the source of that beautiful sound. It may have been this exact bell. She didn't know. She could only imagine what it looked like. She'd seen pictures of bells like this, but she imagined the one she had heard as bigger and more beautiful. Unfortunately, that wonderful child's imagination had not lived long before it became tainted, just like it was now.

This was the first time she had thought about her childhood since the abusive demons sent her away from home. With her now spending most of her time in the street, Jada thought there was no place for happy sounds. It was a place to survive—look out for number one—and to do that, she didn't need childhood memories. She needed determination, strength, and others by her side.

At one point, she thought Seth was all she needed, but he had been taken out of the equation. Now she needed someone else—someone to help her even the score. She had thought that person was Daniel, but she felt betrayed by him. She had done everything he wanted. The priest was disgraced. His message clearly would have no impact with her video evidence of his actions. But as soon as her loyalty was slightly questioned, Daniel appeared ready to throw her like meat to hungry hounds; or in his case, snakes or ravens.

She knew Daniel was capable of this and much more actually. It had been why she wanted Seth to stay away from him, but she decided her plan would work out best with him as her front man. She scolded herself for not playing it smarter. It had all been going so well. Daniel needed someone to humiliate the priest. She needed to get close to the priest's brother.

Maybe it was still working out, she thought. Now she was closer to Louie Castellani than she'd ever imagined she would be. This would be her second chance, and she knew she couldn't afford to screw it up. This time, though, she had loyalty on her side. *Father Marcus…*

She smiled and nodded knowing she was in the right place. She knew this wasn't the first time he had come for her, and now she was in his church. He had given her a bed down here. She was safe and protected even though it felt extremely similar here to where she had come from.

Slowly, something became faintly visible among many short ropes attached to the bell's mounting beam. She watched it not knowing if it was real or just her imagination. She thought it might be just the moonlight playing tricks, and it would go away as fast as it appeared. Within seconds, an opaque shape of a man appeared to be hanging from one of the ropes. That safe feeling she had just been enjoying suddenly disappeared.

Jada anxiously turned back to the door, but she wasn't exactly sure where to go because of the darkness. She rubbed against something soft and loose. She reached for it but stepped on something else. Suddenly, the loose object slapped against her. She grabbed it and immediately realized it was a rope.

The bell clanged once with a deafening echo.

She looked up. The figure was no longer hanging from the rope. Now it was floating down on her like a blanket of comforting protection. It wasn't threatening in any way, but Jada wanted no part of it and tried to get away. With nowhere to go, it engulfed her while she fell to the ground.

Initially she resisted, but soon she felt no need. She lay motionless, unable—unwilling really at this point—to resist.

She watched the figure fade around her. It appeared to be breaking apart, but suddenly it gathered into a cloud then slowly moved under her t-shirt until it was gone.

CHAPTER 25

JADA WOKE TO THE GONG of the church bell—three more—then it stopped. She got up slowly, examining the t-shirt she wore. She had just been sleeping soundly. She knew at least that. Maybe she'd been dreaming too, she thought. She shivered on the edge of the bed—just a mattress on a frame and box spring.

Suddenly, she rushed to a sink and violently vomited. She held on to the sink. In the mirror, she saw her haunting, dark eyes and pale complexion.

She vomited again.

She started to make her way back to the bed but instead, she went to the door and looked into a hallway. She looked in the direction she'd taken during the night but was not anxious to go there again. She heard someone talking beyond light coming from a stairway.

She began walking there and stopped at the bottom of the

stairs. She looked up. She could hear clearly now.

"Look not on our sins, but on the faith of your church, and grant us the peace and unity of your kingdom where you live for ever and ever," she heard Marcus say.

A congregation replied, "Amen."

"The peace of the Lord be with you always."

"And also with you."

She turned away to see the old, damp hallway that appeared to have no ending. Without hesitation this time, she walked down it. This was similar to the hallway she was in during the night, but something about it seemed different to her. She felt the cold and dampness now. She hugged herself as she began to shiver. She felt weak and needed to sit down, but she pressed on to satisfy her curiosity.

Darkness was her destination despite her inability to get there without clinging to the wall for support. Her weakness had turned to dizziness, but she was determined to get closer to something she started to see.

At the end of the hall, she entered another room. This one was bigger than the one she was in before, but it was similar in appearance and completely empty. As soon as she entered, a door within it began to shake. Slowly at first then with increased intensity.

She wasn't frightened by this. She was no longer cold or dizzy either. It just seemed extremely odd to her that a door would shake for no reason. She could see well enough, and there was nothing in here to make her rush out. Instead, she walked to the door and began to unlock it. First the top latch then the bottom.

The door continued to shake then pounding started. That was startling to her at first, but Jada wasn't the type to flee from anything without knowing what she was running from. She took the wooden handle and lifted it.

The shaking—pounding stopped. So did the handle.

She tried to move it but couldn't. She tried with more force. It gave as did the door.

It cleared swiftly past her and slammed against the wall. She was almost knocked down by a strong force of rushing air. It engulfed the room like a violent storm. Jada stood facing the tunnel exposed beyond. Nothing was there, but she knew the look on her face said otherwise.

As quickly as the air had filled the room, it left, nearly sucking Jada into the tunnel. She resisted and the door swung…

CHAPTER 26

A MUFFLED THUD came from the basement as Marcus exited the church with the processional cross. His eyes opened wide, and he staggered a little during his slow pace. He didn't turn around. He just kept moving as though nothing happened.

No one knew he had a girl in the basement, yet. *What the hell was I thinking bringing her here? Or trying to protect her; trying to find her; trying to help her, or… Am I a priest or a youth counselor? Or am I just a seriously demented, sex deprived pervert?*

He sighed knowing others were right behind him. He hoped that single thump in this century old church would be the only one, and it wouldn't get anyone asking questions. Then he wondered what exactly she was doing down there. Did she fall? Was she trying to leave? What would these people do if she came running up the stairs screaming like a captured school girl? He shook his head slightly as he placed the cross into its holder. *Why am I such an idiot? My God, it's just another set-up.*

Then he remembered the look in her eyes when Daniel threatened her life. He had been the only one there for her. They were both in the same situation—doomed if he hadn't done something. He'd gone inside to get answers. He stepped up to Daniel because someone had to. He was right to protect her. He knew he had done the right thing... He closed his eyes and took a soft breath. But he shouldn't had gone there in the first place. This is where he belonged, and if he had been here...

He closed his eyes and continued to receive his congregation of five.

CHAPTER 27

STILL IN HIS SILK CHASUBLE, Marcus stood at the top of the stairs contemplating if now was the right time to confront Jada. He knew he had to, but her answers worried him as much as how he would ask the questions he needed answers to.

He heard commotion where he dreaded going. She was moving. She crashed into something. Then he heard her vomiting—dry heaves. It was obvious she'd done it many times before. He knew she needed someone to help her, but his back was in the air again. She was the enemy, and she was in his basement.

When she needed him before, he didn't hesitate. He had been quick to be the hero and save the damsel in distress. But that was when she had no one to turn to. Now her threat was gone, and back in full force was Marcus's rage against her.

He knew he should be mainly concerned about what he

had done to that kid, not what she had done to him. The kid was dead and he, the new priest in town, was responsible. It was self-defense, he tried to convince himself. He had a gun, and he had no choice other than to use it.

Explaining it all was something he preferred not to do. He knew too well the ramifications of turning himself in. Although his past teachings as a priest told him it would be the right thing, his instincts that came from the streets left that option completely off the table.

What would happen next was a more relevant question to Marcus. Others were there, and although they may not have seen him pull the trigger, they would surely point that gun in his direction. Maybe nothing would be said from that group at all, he thought. Considering what was going on in there, possibly this would just go down as another missing persons case.

Then he thought of Jada again. She had seen the fight. She had heard the blast. She had watched the gun fall from Marcus's hand. He stared down the stairs then grabbed for the wall. His legs trembled as he fell short of breath. She betrayed him before. Why wouldn't she do it again? He turned away and paused before walking back toward the church.

CHAPTER 28

MARCUS HESITATED AT THE DOOR of the room he had given to Jada. He was no longer dressed as a priest. Now he looked just like any other guy which was the farthest thing from how he actually felt. *Why can't I live a mundane life just like anyone else or any other priest for that matter?*

He entered the room to find Jada clinging to the sink. He put a glass of water beside the bed then went to help her. "Come on," he said. He guided her back to the bed where she curled up, apparently looking for warmth and comfort. He offered neither.

He was confused at this point. He knew he needed her on his side. He needed to keep her close, so he would know what she was doing and saying. But he had trouble finding the ability within himself to keep her here.

He got the water and sat with her. "Here, you have to drink."

She lifted her head and looked at him but said nothing. She took the glass and after taking a drink, she said, "Where's Grace?"

He hadn't thought much about Grace since he agreed to bring Jada back here. She could help him. She seemed to care about more than just herself. "She'll be back." At least he hoped she would be.

He got up and turned away from her. He approached a bookcase that was mostly filled with old, dusty bibles. He touched one hoping it would help him find some sense in all of this. "Why, Jada?"

"Sorry. The devil made me—"

He turned back to her sharply. She was almost laughing and turned away with a smart ass smirk.

"Forget it," she said.

"You think it's a joke? You tape me... And now I've killed someone. That's a joke to you?"

"Sorry."

"Sorry! What the hell is that? I need more than sorry, Jada." He turned away and banged his arm against the wall. "I need a reason, an excuse, something." He turned back holding on to his forehead. He saw her watching him, but she seemed more interested in his reaction than his grief. "Maybe you hate priests, or it's all for him. A prank, a dare, a fuckin' fantasy." He pulled his hand away aggressively and looked directly at her. "Anything, Jada. Anything but sorry."

She looked away with a slight eye roll. "Thanks." She took another drink.

Marcus stared in silence. It didn't bother her at all, he thought. Was it her youth? Was it because of her being on the street? Was she like this to everyone, or was it just because of the white collar he wore? She was a self-centered brat who didn't know how to appreciate a helping hand. No wonder she ended up where she did.

He suddenly realized, it didn't matter anyway. He meant nothing to this girl. Regardless of all he had done to protect her, and the affection she appeared to have toward him, he knew now she was heartless. She had led him on to satisfy her selfish needs. She had made him feel important, so he would do anything when she was backed up against the wall. She sensed his weakness and was a master of manipulating it. But really, he thought, she was just a kid literally fucking with him.

This kid held the key to his future in more ways than one, though, so something would have to make her change. He didn't know how, but if she was going to stay here—even if she didn't—he knew he'd have to find a way.

Having her close was probably best, but he didn't know if, or how long, he could take her games. Sending her away would definitely be the end of him when she found an opportunity to exploit his sins. He had to decide if he would keep her nearby or send her back where she probably belonged.

However, neither of those thoughts dealt with the change that would set him free from Jada's greed, and neither dealt with a dead kid probably still lying in the tunnel.

Grace entered the room carrying a bag. "How is she?" She went directly to Jada and started taking things from the bag. "Your clothes, not mine," Grace said to her. She smiled then turned to Marcus, suddenly serious. "The alley's all taped off." She got up, appearing to inspect the room as though she was considering staying there too. "He was found with a bullet in his chest this morning."

"I didn't think anyone would care," Marcus said. "Certainly no one does here."

Grace looked at Jada. "Normally, that would be true." She gave her a concerned look. Marcus knew she wasn't impressed. "If he was one of us." She turned back to Marcus. "The son of a city councilor gets more respect I guess."

Marcus didn't respond. There was nothing but silence, again...

Marcus knew now neither of them could be here. That would put two street kids in hiding at the church. As soon as someone found out, Marcus would be implicated. But he wasn't just involved, he was guilty. When that guilt was revealed from Jada's lips, the new priest in town would fall like all his predecessors.

Was this always Daniel's plan? Did Daniel wrap himself up in all the other priests' sins? Marcus knew suddenly he not only needed to change Jada, but he also needed a plan to deal with Daniel and save himself.

Marcus turned to leave when he saw Grace look back to her. Jada smiled.

"It's not right, Jada," Grace said.

CHAPTER 29

WHEN GRACE STEPPED INTO THE FOYER from the basement stairs, she stopped and looked at the church entrance. It had been a long time since she'd been in there—walking down that aisle and sitting in those pews. Up until now she had been busy enough to avoid it during the short time Jada had been holed up in the basement. But she had to be sure Jada wasn't going anywhere, and she knew Marcus was in the church. Avoiding it seemed no longer an option, but she thought if she paused long enough, the priest might emerge.

Her problem with going there had nothing to do with the pleasant memories this church gave her. As a child, she came from a close family who spent plenty of time together inside these walls. She had been baptized here. She had her first communion here. She remembered running through this exact room chasing other kids after mass was over. They had all done whatever they could to avoid being quieted by the grown-ups, and they conspired among each other to come up with plans to steal more cookies from the heavily guarded tray. She would have no doubt been married here and brought her new family here, following the same path her parents had set out for her.

All of that changed, however, when Grace decided her family members were a bunch of freaks. She was young then and not much different than any other teenager. She had figured her parents loved Jesus too much, and she became determined to make a point that she wouldn't be following suit. Grace took it too far, though, and her parents packed her bags. She always knew it had been a show of parental authority, but back then Grace took her stuff and never looked back.

She had often wondered why her parents didn't put up an all-out effort to find her. They were exactly the type of people who would have done that. But there was no attempt, at least as far as she knew there wasn't. She wouldn't have gone back even if there was, but knowing she was simply out of sight, out of mind infuriated her beyond explanation.

Much of the anger she had against her parents had been taken out on this church. It seemed like a good thing to do back then, but now she realized it had just been immature. Everything they did was, though, so destroying a church seemed extremely appropriate.

Just like Jada, the groups she had been with during her days as a street kid followed the words of Daniel. She had never let her beliefs sink that low, but she didn't hesitate to be involved in their actions against St. Paul's Catholic Church. The raids; the vandalism; the hate... Grace had been part of it all. It wasn't until she started to speak out against Daniel that she realized the damage they had caused.

When she had heard of the new priest, she hoped her cause might actually get a boost. His message would be from the church; hers from the street, but they would both be communicating against the likes of Daniel. The only thing required was for some to change their way of thinking. Others would follow, then others, and before long...

She'd heard the church was being rebuilt. She'd seen the flyer of the first mass. Then the name, Castellani. Father Marcus Castellani... Louie Castellani... Jada and her obsession to avenge Seth's murder...

Shit, she thought. *Now I have to face my destructive past in order to solve a disastrous future. Why do I sign up for this shit?*

She shook her head to clear those thoughts and started her walk of shame toward the century old church door.

When she entered, the refinished beauty was breathtaking. It was almost exactly as she remembered it. She couldn't believe she had been involved in its destruction. The only thing different was that it was actually better now. Maybe that was because she was old enough to appreciate all this place had to offer. Maybe it was that her hope was suddenly restored. Maybe the new priest was the reason. Despite all the roadblocks ahead, if Father Marcus Castellani could do what he did here, maybe he could do the same everywhere.

She saw Marcus praying in a pew. She walked down the aisle. "I have to go back out," Grace said.

Marcus didn't look up. "Is she sick or just possessed?"

"Don't know." *Trust me, I really don't.*

"She has to go."

"Just until she gets better, please. I've been trying to get her away from Daniel for a long time. At least that's happened."

He looked back at her with tears in his eyes. "At my expense. Now, what's the cost for my redemption, Grace?"

***

GRACE walked out from the church. As she moved down the walkway toward the sidewalk, an unmarked police car pulled up to the curb. She knew right away it was a cop, and she thought immediately that he was after her. Her street instincts were suddenly on full alert. She looked quickly both ways to get her surroundings straight. She couldn't run—that would be crazy, but as a last resort... She'd done nothing wrong. She knew of those who had, but how could this guy know that?

She kept moving, and walked straight toward the driver's door. She got a good look at him before she turned away. Much to her surprise, she was not confronted as she made her way down the sidewalk. When she felt cleared of any suspicion, she looked back and memorized the license plate.

CHAPTER 30

MARCUS DIDN'T LOOK UP from cleaning the altar when he thought he heard Grace. "I just have to look out for myself, Gra—" He looked up. A man stood at the doors, not Grace.

"My thought exactly about my life. I assumed you would try to change that." He smiled. "I let myself in. Hope you don't mind."

Marcus straightened up, startled to see someone else there. "Sorry, but Mass was at eleven." He sighed at the thought of actually wanting to send this guy away. It was hardly the way to build a lasting relationship, but the timing… *Why do things always work out this way?*

The man continued down the aisle. "Thanks, Father, but I'm in way too deep for that." He smiled again. "I'm Detective Monroe. A few questions?"

Marcus knew he showed instant nervousness. *Shit. Someone*

talked. He knows about Jada being here. He closed his eyes to calm himself hoping the detective was too far away to notice. "About wha—" He cleared his throat. "Sorry, about what?" *Great. If he can't see me trembling, the first words out of my mouth pretty much sums it up.*

Detective Monroe got closer. "A murder, Father." He walked slowly, closer still. "Last night a young man—a teenager—was murdered downtown."

"Downtown? Why me?" *Instant denial. What else would I do? He's probably got a cruiser waiting outside already.* "I don't mean to sound unconcerned, but what has that got to do with me?"

"Well, our records have you being questioned around where it happened a few nights ago." The Detective waited for a response. "Been hangin' out with any—"

And that was with my brother. He no doubt knows his history and my past. "No, sir, I haven't."

"Were you downtown last night, Father?" He followed that statement with a piercing stare.

"No," Marcus replied.

Detective Monroe stopped. Marcus said nothing more.

"You sure, Father Marcus… Castellani?"

Now, he was too close for any unnoticed expressions. A confession was right on the tip of Marcus's lips. *Maybe it's best that way. I can claim self-defense; expose Daniel and his activity.* He shook his head slowly and looked down. *I can watch myself wash away—gone and forever forgotten, just like the others.*

He knew right then this was Daniel's plan. Daniel didn't do anything about Marcus in the room because he knew the kid would do it for him. If the kid didn't take Marcus out, this would likely result which would be much better than a simple sex tape.

"Not lookin' for a late night fix? A gun at the scene could—"

The door opened behind Detective Monroe. Marcus looked up quickly. Father Burke stepped in from the back of the church.

"He was with me."

Detective Monroe turned.

"Last night, Father Marcus was with me," Father Burke repeated.

No I wasn't...

"And you're?"

"I'm Father Burke, Marcus's Bishop."

"He was with you? All night?"

"Yes, sir, all night."

No, not even for one minute... In fact I haven't seen you for quite a while, and I didn't know you were coming by anytime soon. Please tell me you haven't been downstairs.

Marcus watched nervously as Detective Monroe stared the Bishop down. Father Burke didn't flinch. Detective Monroe turned back to Marcus. Marcus didn't move either.

"Alright then, thanks for your time, gentlemen. If I have more questions—"

Marcus breathed a slow sigh of relief as the detective turned away. Marcus could tell, however, he wasn't convinced.

"Feel free to come back anytime. Masses nightly at seven, right, Father Marcus? Sundays at eleven are the most popular."

Marcus didn't answer. He didn't know what would be the right thing to say anyway. *Anything you say could be used...* He knew this could turn against him anytime, and Father Burke had handled it perfectly. *But why?*

He watched Detective Monroe walk back up the aisle and confront Father Burke. He didn't move, forcing the Detective to go around. Detective Monroe looked back to Marcus with a look that almost stopped his blood running, but not Father Burke's. He followed the detective out.

Father Burke shut the doors and turned back. "Marcus, you can't run a hostel in the basement."

Shit. He has been downstairs. Marcus nodded. "Did I make it longer than the others?" *And now that you've got a church back, I hope you've got another sucker lined up to run this freak show.*

Father Burke sat down in a nearby pew. "Well, you're much better looking."

His slight smile indicated that he expected a reaction, but Marcus gave him none. Marcus was unsure why, but he felt set-up by the Bishop as well as everyone else. He could see in Father Burke's eyes, however, he was not giving up on him.

"You haven't broken any glass, stole from the collection box, stained your ceremonial stole, have you?"

Marcus looked away. *Probably all of the above...*

"What you've got to offer those kids is extremely important, Father Marcus. The girl downstairs is proof of that."

"She's a constant reminder of what I have to offer."

Father Burke got up and slowly began to leave. After a few steps he stopped. He didn't look back. "The Lord wants you to walk as one of his heroes, Marcus. Simply confessing your sins is all that's required."

Man, I doubt even you're ready for that.

Father Burke left.

CHAPTER 31

IT WAS NO LONGER A QUESTION if Jada was going to stay. It simply came down to how Marcus would kick this problem kid back onto the street. When he had been out there, he always had a home to go to. Jada didn't have a home, but she certainly wasn't going to make one here.

He knew now his only chance of getting that detective off his back was to get Jada as far away from this church as he possibly could. His problem was actually doing it. Any other time, he didn't feel like he had it within himself to do something like that. He'd been there. He knew what it was like for these kids. In this case things were different, though. With all of his doubt put aside, he was confident it would happen now.

He grabbed the handle on the door of the room Jada was in. He hesitated and turned away. *Dammit!* His words weren't clear in his head. He'd rehearsed what he would say. He'd acted out his presentation, but something didn't feel right. Maybe he needed more time to think this through. Possibly, there was another way... He leaned against the wall, but only for a second.

The answer was clear. With Jada gone and Father Burke's alibi, he was free from all of this. He was sure of it. All he had to do was stay here in the church and continue doing what Father Burke brought him here to do. They're not going to put a priest at that crime scene. Just because he was questioned near there before didn't make him a murderer. And as far as Louie goes, he didn't have any charges against him as far as Marcus knew. *For all they know, he's my bloody altar boy.*

He approached the door again with his confidence soaring. He pushed it open but stopped. *By the way, Father Burke saying I was with him... He has no idea, or does he?*

When he stepped into the room, Jada was sitting up in bed with Grace beside her. "You're better?"

That was not part of the script... He looked closely at her, and she really did look better. *At least I'm not kicking her out when she can barely walk. At least she's got Grace, so she really does have somewhere to go. At least for now.*

"She stopped puking," Grace responded.

Awesome. She probably wants to go anyway. Surely, a girl like Jada has no interest in being holed up in the basement of a nineteenth century church. If she truly was better, she would be leaving. He knew she would, and Grace was here to make it happen. He wouldn't have to say a thing. *Any second now they'll both get up and...*

Grace looked at Jada. "We know what's wrong."

And you can take her with you to get that taken care of. "Really." *Perfect timing.*

Grace got up and went to the sink. She took a thin strip of plastic and held it up. "She's pregnant."

CHAPTER 32

WHEN MARCUS STEPPED into the backyard, he saw Angelica struggling with something just inside the door of her garden shed. He knew what she was doing. It was exactly the time of year for it, but the neighborhood didn't seem to be up for this type of thing anymore. His mother was different than most, and he was delighted to see what he hadn't since he'd been gone. He assumed she hadn't missed even one year of putting up Christmas lights since his father died.

He remembered how anxious he used to be at this time of year. The lights were the beginning of the season for him, and getting his father to put them up had been first on his list of Christmas activities. He thought about how annoying that must have been, but his father never put up much of a fight. He would just put aside whatever he was doing, and together they would work on the tangled strings and put up the same display year after year.

Back then, the community seemed to rise up to celebrate Christmas. Lights decorated houses on all the streets. Sidewalks were always filled with anxious shoppers. His parents made plans they had never typically made during any other time of the year. Marcus couldn't help himself from getting caught up in it all.

That was until his father died. After that, Marcus had nothing to do with Christmas lights, or the tree, or gatherings, or presents... He didn't remember caring anymore. He took to a life on the street with the advantage of having a place to sleep. But Angelica kept doing the lights. When Marcus would come home at whatever time, he was always shocked by the sight of them. He remembered it bringing back memories he often found hard to shake off.

When his street life was over, he went straight to the seminary. He hadn't been back for Christmas until now, and by the looks of it, his mother hadn't forgotten about the lights even if the rest of the community had.

Marcus asked, "If I offer to help, do you promise they won't attack?"

She turned with a tangled mess. "Oh. Hi, Marcus." She held them up in front of her. "I don't remember putting them away like this."

"Then Louie must have done it," he said.

She smiled sarcastically. "I'm sure the thought of anything remotely like this has never crossed his mind." She thought for a second. "I wouldn't say the same about you, though. I hope you haven't forgotten."

Marcus shook his head with a tight-lipped smile. "Everyone else seems to have. I haven't seen a single house with any on yet."

She put down the lights and closed the door. "It's not the same as it used to be, Marcus. Everything has changed over the years. But it only takes one match to start a flame." She smiled. "Shouldn't you be at the church?"

"Yeah, Ma." He paused not sure how to continue. "That's kinda why I'm here." He looked sympathetically at her. "A mother's work is never done."

She gave him a short smile. "Oh, Marcus, I'm too old for cleaning, or cooking, or volunteering. Surely, you can find someone else. Can I make a donation instead?"

Ummm, not quite what I had in mind. He smiled back. "Well, it's—I just need to bring someone here for a while. Until she gets well. I couldn't think of a better place." *And this is a much better place than where she is now.*

"I'm not taking in boarders, Marcus. I never have. I don't want that." She turned away. "Marcus, please. There are all kinds of places for that."

"She's a teenager… She's on the street." He paused, questioning if he should say anymore, but he figured she could read his next words right in his eyes. He wasn't ready for that. She definitely wasn't… At some point the time would come when he would have to tell her but now wasn't it. Just leave it alone, he thought. *She's a teenager. She needs help, and I'll go somewhere else to find it.* That's what his mother wanted, and that's what he should have done in the first place.

But this couldn't be a better place for Jada and for him. "She's pregnant," he said without time to talk himself out of it anymore.

Angelica was shocked. He was right. She wasn't ready for that. She took a step back to balance herself against the shed. He worried that it was too much for her to process. He should have been more sensitive. He knew the dead air between them wasn't doing any good either, but the look on her face indicated she required no further explanation.

CHAPTER 33

MARCUS KNEW BY THE SMELL at the front door that this was probably a good time for introductions. He stepped into the kitchen. Jada hid behind him.

Angelica worked at the counter with a ten quart stockpot brewing on the stove. When she was cooking, she was generally happy. She often showed on the surface that she was in a good mood, but Marcus knew that wasn't always the case. He'd been concerned about her after the news he hit her with the last time he was here.

Marcus said, "Ah, that smell. It's—"

Angelica continued working. "Minestrone this time." She turned. "Hope you like—"

"This is Jada, Ma."

She stood partially covered by Marcus with a shy, insecure smile. Marcus moved away, exposing her. He knew his mother wouldn't accept any half-truths. If she was going to take care of Jada, she would want to see all of what she was getting herself into.

Instantly, Angelica looked like she had just gotten her first Christmas present. Marcus was surprised by her reaction but delighted just the same. He had thought the introduction would be awkward. He knew his mother would make her feel welcome, but he had been concerned about her being forced into this. That assumption couldn't have been further from reality. Angelica was ecstatic to see her—like Jada was a friend's child she hadn't seen since birth.

Angelica smiled and left the counter to greet her. "My, my, I thought—"

She looked at Marcus. He thought her reaction was wrong or deliberately overacted. That, or he'd missed something. Maybe she had thought it over and decided she should be helping her son out. That was what he had hoped for when he asked her, but she was over the top happy now. No one her age would be this pleased about having a street kid over for dinner, and for another dinner, and another...

"You're showing. How far along are you? You must be at least four months, dear." Angelica didn't hesitate to hold Jada's stomach with both hands. She looked back to Marcus with a delighted smile.

Marcus stood shocked. He looked down at Jada's small stomach that he hadn't noticed until now. How could it be, he thought? A week, maybe two, but four months? He struggled with the math, but there was no way it was going to add up.

He turned away to conceal the expression he knew was on his face. *Son of a bitch! This chick will stop at nothing.* There was only one explanation he could come up with. He didn't know what would motivate her to do this, or what she thought she could possibly get out of it. *Does she really think she can hook a priest up with someone else's kid? Is it sheer desperation? She could have picked anyone, but she picked a priest. Is she just letting the cards fly then waiting to see how they land?*

She must have known all along, he thought. It wasn't some great discovery in the basement of the church. That would mean Grace was in on it too. He looked back at Jada, still with his mother, and thought about that. He could see this type of thing coming from Jada, but not Grace. He didn't know Grace well, but he knew her type. She was a lot like him. She was out to help people, not tear them down like so many had been around here. If that was the case—if she was working with the same intent as Marcus, he didn't think she could go through with it.

But if this wasn't another set-up; if it was Marcus's, how could she possibly be four months pregnant? Maybe his mother was wrong. Some women show before others, he was sure of it. He thought hard about what would make him so sure, though. He had no facts about pregnancy. His certainty was simply based on his need for an explanation, and most likely the best answer for that was this whole thing was a scam.

He really didn't know. He was shocked. He was confused. But his mother was delighted, and she was fully onboard. He thought that was all he could handle right now. He needed Jada away from the church. He needed that detective away from both of them. If it was his kid, he would deal with that. If it was someone else's, better. Regardless of whose it was, she also needed to be off the street, so he decided to let it be and find out the details later.

Angelica helped her to a chair at the table. "You must have gone through so much already and without a father." She looked at Marcus. "Well, you've got a priest. Close, I guess." She smiled, but she was the only one.

Marcus really didn't know where to turn. He had been convinced the kid was his, but now… He had decided to get Jada away from him, but she was here—right in his kitchen. She would probably take up sleeping in his bed. Marcus's confusion had him looking like a stranger in his own home.

CHAPTER 34

IN OBVIOUS PAIN, Jada lay in bed with both hands holding her stomach. This pregnancy thing had come on so fast she hadn't even thought about what to expect. She knew little about being pregnant. Sickness was something she'd heard about, and she had been through it already. Hopefully she wouldn't have to deal with that anymore, but what else should she be concerned about? She did know this rapid growth thing she was experiencing simply was not normal.

She looked down at her belly and shook her head in disbelief. It was bigger now than yesterday. How was she supposed to make any sense out of that? Maybe it was okay, she thought. Maybe it would grow in spurts. She really didn't know. She never experienced this with anyone else, and she had no one in her life to tell her any different. But she wasn't stupid either.

One thing she did know about this whole mess was that

Marcus was the father. She hadn't been with anyone else since Seth, and she hadn't wanted to be. She wasn't all that sure about Daniel's plan for her to get with Marcus, but it seemed harmless at the time. She decided it would help her keep Daniel close, so Marcus became her only lover since Seth. This she knew for sure, but there was that creepy thing that happened in the bell tower.

When she had woken up after that, she thought it must had been a dream. She had never been a believer of anything supernatural. She never had any reason to be, but she'd seen some strange stuff happen with Daniel, so nothing seemed too far out of reach. "Jesus Christ," she said to herself. "Isn't a kid enough?" She quickly wiped a tear from her cheek. She should have taken her own advice she had given to Seth and stayed the fuck away from Daniel, she thought.

Her thinking about Seth made her realize how long it had been. She missed him, and she wished this was his. She also realized he was why this had all happened. Her focus had been on Louie Castellani. Her focus had to stay on Castellani. She needed to forget about being pregnant and get back to that. She was in his house now. Any second he could walk through that front door. When that happened blood would fly, and there wouldn't be any coming out of her.

She got up and sat on the edge of the bed. She had to know where the rooms were in this house. She had no excuses to screw this up. This was a small enough place, and he would definitely come here. When her time came with Castellani, she didn't plan on any epic face to face showdown.

Her revenge would be quick and come from any angle. It didn't matter to her how she did it as long as Louie Castellani paid for murdering Seth. He had done it in cold blood, and his payback would be the same.

She stood up and examined her shape. She shook her head realizing how hard it would be not to focus on this. By the looks of it, hunting down Castellani would get harder as time went on, so she was determined to make it happen the first chance she got. She had to find a weapon. A knife was all she needed. He wouldn't even see her coming if she played it right. She just wanted to be sure he knew it was her who made the final plunge. She looked around the room she was in. It was small and the door was closed. She went to it.

In the hallway she saw two other bedrooms and a bathroom. Nothing tough about this layout, she thought. The kitchen was the other way, down the hall. She could tell from the noise Marcus's mother was making there. Blending in with her is what she had to do.

She remembered Marcus saying her name was Angelica. She had to remember that. She had to accept all she offered and become her best friend; her pet project. She rolled her eyes at that thought, but as long as Castellani wasn't here, she knew she would have to play it that way. *When he shows up, that's when the game changes.*

Again, Angelica worked when Jada walked in. Angelica turned but continued at the counter. "You're feeling better?"

"Would be if this thing would stop growing."

"Well it's going to grow, and it's going to move. Trust me

for what it's worth, this is the easy part."

Angelica put her things down and pulled out a chair at the table. "Come, dear. Sit down."

Jada obeyed. *So here it comes. Tell me about how much of a shit I am, and how it's time to pick up my stockings or whatever these old people say.* This is what Jada had worried about when she found out she would be coming here. Being told what to do, and getting advice or direction from anyone other than herself, was something she didn't handle well. Even hearing shit coming from Grace pissed her off, but she would simply have to play along this time. She didn't have to act on it, but she had to listen and pretend she cared.

Angelica continued, "At least I'll do what I can to make it easier for you."

Angelica gave her a warming smile. *Not quite what I was expecting for an opening line.* Jada looked away realizing how easy it would be to screw up with this caring woman being Castellani's mother. And of course, there was Marcus too...

"An Italian kitchen is the perfect place for a pregnant woman." Angelica went to the fridge. "I gained sixty pounds with Marcus." She looked back. "And just like him—" She looked at herself. "It's still with me."

That was a joke. Chuckle or at least smile. Jada did neither. "You give him a place worth coming back to." She watched Angelica getting emotional.

"Not you? You don't have such a place?" Angelica turned away.

Jada saw her wipe her cheek. "If I showed up at the front

door of that place looking like this, I'm not sure who he'd kill first." She watched Angelica shake her head with a sniff.

Angelica closed the fridge. "Come."

She held out her hand. Jada was reserved but took it. *Remember, if she wants to dance, then dance. If she pulls out a Scrabble board, then play Scrabble.* Actually, none of this was bothering Jada much. It was nice not having to spend every minute thinking about where to get something she could fill up on, or worry about who would take what she already had. Angelica walked her out of the kitchen and into the living room.

It was a nice place according to Jada. Dated, but who was she to judge. Since leaving the disaster she called home and living on the street, she hadn't thought much about what she missed in terms of living space. She knew there were other alternatives than living without a roof, but those solutions always came with a catch. The bottom line with shelters and hostels—even boarding houses when she was lucky enough to be at one for free—there was never any intent to keep her within those walls. Their goal was always to find a way to get her back home. The street guaranteed her against that.

Grace's place gave her a hint of something better, but she never let that get in the way of her plans against Castellani. This place was better still in two ways—it was nicer than Grace's, and she could almost smell Louie Castellani.

When she snapped out of her thoughts about housing, she found herself still attached by the hand to Angelica and in front of the mantle looking at pictures.

"Marcus was gone so long. Eight years you know to become a priest."

"And the first thing he did is come back to you?"

"Well, it's not as simple as that. His assignment was St. Paul's"

Jada raised her eyebrows. "He might have been better off having to cook for himself." *My joke right back at ya.* She wondered what type of reaction that would get, but really she didn't care. *Bet she smiles and chuckles, both.* She realized she had to be careful, though. Sarcastic comments weren't going to do her any good, but she had trouble resisting.

Angelica smiled. "It used to be a wonderful place." She chuckled. "Maybe he can bring all of that back. Not just how beautiful it was to look at. He's already done that. He wants to make it like before—a place for you and—" Angelica looked down at Jada's stomach forcing Jada to do the same.

Angelica picked out a picture of Marcus and Louie as kids. She held it like treasure. "Those were times worth remembering. Marcus was wonderful with his father."

Jada asked, "Who's he with?" She knew the answer.

"His brother. He lives here too."

I know that.

"Well kinda. He just comes and goes as he pleases."

Perfect... Jada stood there, politely taking it all in.

CHAPTER 35

LOUIE SAT CASUALLY IN THE DRIVER'S SEAT
of his foreign ride while he cruised down a quiet road that
was well tucked into this damaged neighborhood. Trees that
lined both sides left the potential for a pleasant street, but the
season had already stripped away the leaves. What remained
was just more of the same. To Louie, none of that mattered.
His life had never included any of the wonderful things the
world had to offer. He just knew of bare trees and burnt out
lawns, leaving beautiful landscaping to billboards that lined
the highways.

He was aware he was going too fast, but that didn't bother
him either. He didn't see anyone who would care. Usually,
there would be someone but not this time. He locked his eyes
on to the driveway he was headed for. He could do another
fishtail entry like he'd done so many times before, but today
he wasn't up for it. He wasn't high on anything. No old guy

SINS OF A PRIEST

was there to shake anything at him, so he figured, *what's the point.*

He turned into Angelica's driveway and stopped abruptly. He stayed there for a minute with the music blaring. He hadn't been here in a while and a lot less since Marcus got home. He couldn't think of any particular reason why, but something was not quite the same. It must have been about losing some of the authority he used to have here. Possibly it was a fear of being discovered, but that shouldn't be much of a surprise to Marcus. Regardless, maybe this was the right time to consider a permanent relocation, he thought.

The problem with that was he would end up deeper in a world he needed to get away from sometimes. This is where he came for that, and of course, nothing beat the cooking. But now when he came home for an Italian feast, he usually ended up at the table having to defend his lifestyle. He thought he needed to be in the right place emotionally for verbal showdowns with his brother. He hadn't always been prepared, and he was definitely at a disadvantage since he was against two now. He didn't care much about losing any arguments. All he really wanted to do was present the other side, and to do that he needed to be sharp; definitely not high.

Well, he wasn't high now, and he was starving, so relocation plans would have to wait. If he was lucky, and he'd timed it right, the meal would be ready. He would let out a few smart ass comments and would hit the road again after a good old fashioned dine n' dash. He cut the music, got out, and went straight to the front door.

Louie entered and headed for the kitchen. "Ma. I need to eat." No one was there. *Damn, all that mind prep, and the place is empty.* "Hey, Ma." He went to the living room; no one. "Shit. What's gonna fill the pit now?" He thought he could make something himself, but that idea only lasted for a second. It was much easier to put that task on someone else, even if he had to pay for it.

Suddenly, the agenda in his mind changed. He quickly went to the hallway and directly to his bedroom. He threw a roll of money on the bed along with some small bags of cocaine. The inventory he carried with him was low, so he might as well stock up for some evening action if he wasn't going to stay here. This was the other thing being here was good for. *It's like a vault with an open door.* He smiled at his indulgence while he continued going through his stuff.

Apart from the racket he made, there was a noise from another room. At first he thought otherwise, but he couldn't convince himself. He stopped what he was doing and listened. He heard nothing, but he instinctively gathered his stuff anyway. "Marcus, good—" He went back into the hallway. He stuck his head into Marcus's room. "Didn't think you got time off." There was no one in the room. He looked down the hall then stopped completely. He would have known if someone was here by now because the house was small. Neither Marcus nor Angelica would be this quiet if they were here.

The trigger in his head suddenly went red. Every street

thug had the ability to smell something wrong, and Louie was no different. He'd been in this situation before. It didn't scare him a bit, and no one would be ambushing him, especially in his own house. This was the type of thing Louie excelled at. Sure this was his mother's house, he thought, but when the sirens go off, *it's showtime.*

He flew back to his room and went directly to his second bottom drawer. Quickly, he took out more money and many small bags of blow. He felt through the clothes and found a knife.

Everything went into his pockets except the knife which he extended with the precision of a street pro. Again, he slowly entered the hallway. *Move again, fucker.* He listened precisely. He took a few more cautious steps, but this time a foot kicked his hand that held the knife. It twirled away, penetrating the wall.

He spun around to see Jada standing in a doorway holding a cooking knife. She thrust it toward him which he easily dodged. He looked at his knife stuck in the wall. It was too far away. She tried again, but this time she got too close. He threw her against the wall.

She fell, dropping the knife. He kicked it down the hallway and grabbed his knife from the wall. With a swift turn, he sliced it toward her, just missing her neck, then planted it into the floor.

He was directly over top of her when the front door opened.

***

WHAT Marcus suddenly saw took him a few seconds to process. Jada was defensive against the wall. Louie was in front of her, ready to pounce. A knife lay within reach of Marcus. Another knife was stuck in the floor. There was no blood that he noticed, yet. It was obvious this would escalate almost certainly in Louie's favor, but now the scene was suspended—frozen in time.

Louie turned slowly away from her and faced Marcus for an imminent confrontation. Marcus was in no way ready for this. He could tell by the look on Louie's face, though, time was not an option.

He watched Jada back away, but she only ended up pushing herself against the wall while holding her stomach. Marcus noticed she had the same distressed look as when she was in dire straits with Daniel. It was hard for him to ignore it, even though he thought he had that figured out about Jada. If history repeated itself, which he was sure it would, trouble would surely follow if he defended her. But this time it was different. This was with Louie. These two obviously had some unsolved issue they needed to fight out, and it didn't look like Jada would win the wrestling match.

He saw Jada wince in pain as she held her stomach tighter. Marcus took a few steps forward and stopped with the cooking knife at his feet. "A pregnant woman, Louie? Surely you're not that much of a low life ass—"

"Shit, man! She came flyin' at me with that fuckin' thing."

Marcus looked at the knife. "For no reason?" He looked at Jada. *And what reason would that be?* He shook his head. *At least now I know why there's so much interest in me.* He blasted himself for not seeing this coming after witnessing these two in the street.

"She busted into the place to ice me."

"Why?" Marcus calmly bent over to pick up the knife, but he stopped and left it where it was.

"What the fuck, man. Do you know who—"

"Yeah, Louie, I know who she is. She's with me."

Louie was obviously confused. He looked back at her. Marcus knew exactly what was going through his head. What Louie thought about this pregnant kid made no difference. In Marcus's mind, the baby was his. He knew there was a chance it wasn't, but this was not the time to beat himself up over that. He wasn't just defending Jada this time. He was defending his own, and it was against his brother of all people.

Louie continued, "I thought you were a—"

Marcus stepped toward him.

"Marcus, come on! We're blood, man."

"Blood? You sure that's what runs through your veins, Louie? And why does she want to cut you open to set it free?"

"Ten grand meant more to you than his life," Jada said directly to Louie. "Strange isn't it? Now I feel the same way about you."

Marcus took another step toward him. He didn't get the

whole picture with that, but he knew instantly it was about money and someone's life. He cringed knowing now just what kind of street thug his brother had become. He'd seen this kind before, and he had stayed far away from them. The fact that his brother had become the same as those he used to fear, made him realize he never should have let him out of his sight.

Jada continued, "With a blade in your eye, we'll call it even."

Louie started to back up. "What, man, for this piece of shit?"

Now Marcus was too close for Louie to do anything except grab the knife stuck to the floor and defend himself. Marcus knew he would fall first if he let it go any further. Louie was the type who acted fast with a weapon in his hand. Judging by the length of time Louie had been on the street, he would handle the blade much better, so a fight like this was basically already over.

Marcus looked down at the cooking knife. He kicked it away. He looked back to Louie and slowly went to take his knife. Louie resisted at first but handed it over.

"Only because of who you are, bro. Anyone else and it would be in ya by now," Louie said.

No use arguing about that. Marcus dropped it also, then with extreme accuracy, he drifted Louie in the face.

Louie recovered and rushed him. They slammed against the wall, but Marcus got an elbow to Louie's chin. *But there is a point to showing who's who around here.*

Louie was slower to respond. Marcus stood over him waiting.

Another intruder entered the house. Marcus looked away to see Angelica at the door. *Shit!* Just as he expected, she reacted like any Italian mother would when she saw her two boys fighting.

"Voi due bastardi! (Bastards, the two of you!)," she screamed. She went straight to Jada. "We get a girl in the house and see what happens." She helped her up. "You okay, dear?" She stared at Louie. "You—always a disappointment."

Marcus watched her with a hand raised, intending to slap him, but she didn't. She must have thought Marcus had already taken care of that, or she realized how bad of an idea that might be.

Louie got back on his feet. He slammed Marcus with a look of hate that even these brothers may not be able to recover from. He turned away, hammered the wall, and left.

Marcus wasn't sure if he should chase after him or let him go. There was really no point in Louie being here now. Jada seemed to want him just as dead as he wanted her to be. Who knew what she would do given another chance.

Angelica's attention turned to Jada who now winced in pain. Marcus watched her examine Jada's stomach. He noticed it was considerably bigger than the last time he'd seen her. With that, and the thought that he'd convinced himself it was his, he was suddenly extremely concerned.

"Marcus, when's the last time she saw a doctor?"

Marcus said nothing. He just wrinkled his face and forced

his eyes closed with both hands.

"Where's your family, dear?" he heard Angelica say.

CHAPTER 36

IN THE BACKLIT STREET BEYOND, an active nightlife contrasted heavily with the dismal atmosphere Daniel watched it from. He played the role of a heavily disguised bum because he knew the person he waited for would recognize him otherwise. Probably, this wouldn't fool her either, but it just made sense considering his vantage point was beside an overflowing garbage bin. Dangling from it, and somewhat concealing his position, was yellow barrier tape: "*POLICE LINE DO NOT CROSS.*"

He pulled on the tape because it was more of a distraction than camouflage. He looked at the piece in his hand. He smiled with the thought of the events that caused this to be here. If it wasn't for the threat the priest represented, that night would have been perfect entertainment for his group of prestigious satanic worshippers. As it turned out, the wrong person paid the ultimate price, and any gift of sacrifice was meaningless with the priest's harsh departure. He had the kid dropped out here, and one of Daniel's decorated followers was left reeling with the conscious dilemma of birth blood versus faith. He knew, however, in time faith would win, and his VIP trooper would come back with a renewed lust for the cause. Hopefully, that would include a thirst for revenge that the priest would have to deal with too.

That wasn't Daniel's problem now, though. He was specifically concerned with the priest. Daniel didn't have time to wait for others to come around. Since his apprentice appeared to have jumped ship, now he was left with the disposing of this pest himself. Having Jada as an eager volunteer was a luxury he surely enjoyed, but his current dilemma could certainly be served well with her even through unwillingness. It was Jada he would continue using because he knew wherever she was, the priest would follow if he wasn't already there.

He shifted slightly in his hobo's nest, fully prepared to wait this out for however long it took. He knew he didn't have to go far to find his direct lead to Jada. Jada was no longer in with the crowd he would typically depend on for ratting her out, but close by was an even better source. This girl had been a problem for Daniel for quite some time, but he always knew her annoyance would come in handy at some point. That moment was now, and whether she knew it or not, she would soon give up what Daniel knew she was hiding.

He looked quickly to the active street then back to his

fixation. He watched Grace's apartment where a single light shone.

CHAPTER 37

STILL SQUATTING BESIDE THE GARBAGE BIN, Daniel had no intention in calling it a day, or night, or morning as time would have it. Not much had changed except now, there was no nightlife, and Grace's light had just been turned off.

Of course, that could have been her just going to bed, but he doubted it. He knew the hours she kept, and Jada wasn't with her. She'd been in that place the whole time Daniel had watched her, so it was more likely she was about to meet up with his target.

Daniel hadn't moved in hours. He tilted his head slightly, anticipating that finally his time had come. There was movement inside but only for a few seconds. Then, as he was sure would eventually happen, Grace stepped onto the fire escape. He watched her run down the stairs and head for the street.

***

GRACE left the alley quickly without even taking a peek to see if he was there. She had just spent hours deciding how to pull off what she was about to do. Planning, phone calls, waiting, all while she knew Daniel lurked for her in the alley.

In her mind, if he was going to follow her, it would be into a trap. But she wasn't ready when the crime scene had been opened up the day before. She had been working on a plan and was now forced to escalate its shaky details.

She had just gotten back into her apartment when she noticed him. She watched for hours to see if he would go away, but he wasn't moving. She knew he had no interest in her, so she wondered what he still wanted with Jada. She had obviously done something that put her on Marcus's side, but Daniel appeared to be still pursuing her to get rid of the priest.

Jada was no longer at the church. She figured he had already gone there and found that out. His alternative plan must be to scare Jada's location out of her or use her as bait. That idea probably would have worked if Grace wasn't thinking one step ahead. She knew she had to act fast, and her hasty decisions would probably fail, but she had a plan now and was about to execute it.

She turned along the sidewalk and stopped in the nearest doorway. A taxi sat at the curb with a sleeping driver. There was usually a line of cabs out here, but it was too late. At least she saw one, and it didn't look like he was going anywhere. She looked down the street satisfied that the time was right. She had waited until the street life would be nonexistent. Across the street, leaning in another dimly lit doorway, she saw Detective Monroe watching her.

She nodded to him. He did the same. Good, she thought. He must have believed her story, or at least he was curious enough to see where this would go. When she first called him, he insisted she come to the station and make a statement. She refused and stuck to her plan to get him here. Hopefully, Daniel was still there, so her next step would go off as planned. She slowly walked back to the alley.

Grace approached the fire escape and paused. "She's not coming back." She waited but nothing happened. She had noticed when she first entered the alley Daniel was no longer part of the garbage collection. She was quite sure he hadn't let her off the hook, though. At a time like this, Daniel was not the type for pleasant greetings. Hiding would be a normal reaction for him. She stepped up to the first flight of stairs. "Ever…"

Nothing moved in the alley, but now something was inches from the back of her neck. She felt heavy breathing that seemed just short of losing control. She almost launched herself up the stairs to the safety of her apartment, but she stayed put. She knew she probably wouldn't have gotten that far anyway.

Daniel said softly in a raspy voice, "Where is she?"

Grace cringed with fear that she tried desperately to

conceal. It wasn't so much the words that frightened her but the emphasis he put on each one. "Where would you think at a time like this?" She felt her body tremble. "With the very person you fear the most," she continued.

She took a deep breath and turned quickly, but he was gone. She wasn't sure if he was actually ever there, right next to her. The words were his, though. That, she knew.

She saw Detective Monroe standing in the entrance. A beam of light flooded the alley from a flashlight he held. The light hit Grace and quickly moved to other parts of the alley. He wasn't supposed to make himself the center of attention, or even visible for that matter. It was enough that she'd been rushed into this, and now she could tell she had partnered with an idiot.

Frustrated, she turned away from him and followed the light. She thought there would be a trace of him, if not Daniel himself standing there, intimidating as the hell he represented. She knew he wasn't afraid of her, and this nut case with the light certainly wouldn't concern him. But nothing—no one was there. The alley looked just as deserted as it would be any other morning at this time.

She turned back to Detective Monroe. He was stepping into the alley, but he was looking beyond her. "The guilty are always hiding. Innocence, never." He stopped. He shrugged at Grace.

Was that statement directed at me, or did you see something I didn't? She was about to ask him out loud, a little less sarcastically, when suddenly a force smashed into him. It wasn't anything physical, just a force. He slammed against the wall. He went for his gun.

"But sometimes, guilt is obvious," Detective Monroe said while fumbling to keep his balance and secure his gun.

She watched the detective searching frantically for what hit him. Grace's plan was to get some type of confession from Daniel which would pin him as the kid's murderer, but it didn't look like that was necessary now. Detective Monroe seemed convinced from this and her word, so despite his stupidity, she was satisfied with the way things were going.

Suddenly, Daniel appeared right in front of her. She didn't know where he came from, but out of nowhere, he was there—like a devilish Vegas act. She could have blinked or possibly the dark was playing tricks on her, but his abilities never ceased to amaze her. They almost impressed her, even if they scared the shit out of her.

She watched the detective begin to rise up the wall against his will. Daniel followed his assent, but he wasn't touching him. This could be just an illusion, she figured, but she could see from the detective's expression he wasn't finding any of this entertaining. As he rose higher, he seemed paralyzed with realistic fear. She wasn't convinced it was an act either. She'd seen strange things from Daniel before. They could easily be shaken off as tricks, but something about all of it—something about him made it feel extremely real. In fact, in her mind it was real, and just the thought of that scared her even more.

Daniel demanded, "Where is she?"

He was staring at the detective, but Grace knew the question was still directed at her. She responded, "Try the church, or is it too much for you when he's there?" She knew that question would insult him, but she had to get him away from Detective Monroe.

"It's Jada I want." Daniel turned to Grace. "Where is she?" His powerful voice echoed between the walls.

"It may be Jada you want, but it's the church you need. Isn't that right, Daniel? It's the only thing you've got now. The Mayan Calendar scare; the Y2K—both failures. What other plans have you got to impress the mightiest of all sinners?" *There, another insult.* She cringed at the thought of his reaction. She shook thinking about what he would do knowing she knew all that. She wasn't a Satanist. She had no right to that information.

She saw Detective Monroe look down with extreme uncertainty. He started trembling when he spoke. "I don't know who the hell Jada is, but you're—"

With nothing touching him, Detective Monroe's face began to squish against the wall. Daniel was inches away. It seemed to Grace he was using the detective as some sort of punching bag—a meaningless object to unleash his growing frustrations on. Grace thought the detective must be witnessing an image of hell that made death a much better alternative.

"Looks like you've failed, again," Grace continued, trying to keep Daniel's attention on her.

Daniel turned abruptly, and he started growing. He

became massive in an extremely small place. Grace stepped back and looked around to be sure there was still somewhere for her to escape. She turned to him again, determined to carry on.

Detective Monroe fell to the ground. He scurried to get back on his feet and rushed toward Grace. "Settin' up a cop—" He looked back for Daniel, terrified. "Is this what the street breeds?"

She knew he was talking to her. He was obviously lost about what was going on, but she had to keep pressing Daniel. "You thought the sinning priest would fall, but it looks like someone has other plans," Grace said.

Detective Monroe rushed to Grace and pushed her toward the entrance. "Move outta here, now!" he commanded.

She brushed him off causing him to lose his balance and fall to his knees. She realized her plan to involve the detective was now completely screwed up. Daniel was raged, leaving any hope for her and the detective almost lost. She had to come up with something else quick, now in fact.

"No plan is more powerful than exposing a priest's sins," Daniel said.

"You're right. Especially when she carries his baby," Grace responded.

After that it was silent—nothing from Daniel, and nothing from Grace. She couldn't believe what she'd just done. She just said it. She didn't plan on it, but the words came out. She instantly tried to think out the ramifications of saying those words. What would happen to Jada? What about Marcus and the church? What would Daniel do to the baby? She cringed at the mistake she'd just made.

Daniel would no doubt have two fires burning now. If he had been after Jada just to get his sights on Marcus, now his plans for her would include the baby. A member of his inner circle pregnant with a priest's child... There wasn't a chance in his cherished hell he would let that continue.

He didn't need to know anything about it. Her plan was to implicate Daniel in the worshipper's death. That was all. That would have distracted him enough to get Jada away from here, but she had to fuel his fire. She closed her eyes knowing she was about to see Daniel's true capabilities.

Daniel's reaction was emotionless at first. He stared at her and tilted his head slightly. For a brief moment she thought he didn't believe her. She expected him to break out in some howling laugh, but she was wrong. His emotionless face went stone cold. He stared death straight at her. Then, a whirlwind of fury erupted. Garbage flew and wind echoed—a hurricane in the alley.

He drove himself forward with full force toward Grace.

"Jada's carrying the child of a holy man... A man of Christianity... A man of Christ," Grace said, determined to push the issue and hold her ground just because she didn't know what else she could do. She turned to see Detective Monroe running for the entrance. "Another wrinkle, Daniel? Unless Christ's presence doesn't concern you," she continued.

Daniel flew past Grace. She stayed put and closed her eyes in relief. She had thought, definitely, those would be her last words. She watched him swoop down and pick up the detective. He was helpless. Daniel began throwing him throughout the alley as though he was riding a roller coaster without tracks.

Daniel stopped in front of Grace. He held the detective like a piece of paper he was just waiting to tear apart. "The priest must pay for his sins. Satan is God, and the priest must fall."

Grace responded, "Or what, Daniel? What happens to world domination with the priest in your way?"

She saw Detective Monroe struggle with his throat. He gulped desperately. He gasped for air. She thought she heard him say something. She noticed Daniel hear it too.

Daniel's fury stopped. "What?"

"The priest is guilty," Detective Monroe said quietly, barely able to speak. He tried to catch his breath. "I have unidentified prints on the gun." He coughed uncontrollably. "Marcus Castellani? He was a gangster kid." He paused to be sure he could continue. "I'm sure they're his."

Grace watched Daniel look down at her and drop the detective. His force tamed. His height returned to normal. He taunted her with a horrendous smile. "Not all sins are forgiven."

She secretly reached into her pocket and slipped out a knife. She flipped it open while holding it close to her side. "You sure?" She knew what she had to do. She had no choice. Her plan had failed horribly, and now Marcus was certainly going to be pinned to the death he'd caused.

She never took her eyes off Daniel, and she knew Detective Monroe stood next to her trying to regain his composure. She tried to come up with another solution, but she couldn't think straight. She was focused on one action that would change Marcus's certain destiny.

She moved swiftly, slashing the knife in the air and cut deep into the detective's throat. He gasped for air with blood gushing then collapsed to the ground.

"She's not coming back," Grace said.

She watched Daniel's rage intensify. She began to run toward the street. She reached the sidewalk. Both sides were completely empty. She wanted someone to be here but realized it was much better this way. She had planned this time so the streets would be empty. She knew she wasn't thinking straight. She had to focus, but she'd just killed a cop for Christ's sake... She saw the taxi still parked up the street and ran directly for it.

She looked back to see Daniel flying from the alley in desperate pursuit. She crashed straight into a garbage can. She scrambled to her feet. She surged for the taxi, barely able to get her footing.

She saw the driver wake up when she hit the door. Grace threw herself in then slammed the door shut. She screamed, "Go, now. Now!"

She watched the driver suddenly turn. He looked out his window. Daniel was now a fury of flame which engulfed the car.

The driver screamed, "Holy, Mother of God!" He started it and floored the gas pedal.

Grace flew sideways in the back seat from the car's harsh departure. She pulled herself up and looked out the back window with the sound of the taxi squealing away.

They left a trail of Daniel's flame behind.

CHAPTER 38

HAVING NOT YET RETURNED to a physical form, Daniel's force burst open the door in the church basement. His ghostly spirit quickly filled the room, and he felt a sense of comfort being back in the place he cherished the most. Sure he had returned after the priest took over, but he hadn't been down here.

This was Daniel's lair. It had been where he conjured up his plans and rested so he could execute them. He was pleased to see it hadn't been disturbed. There were no furnishings and nothing annoying hanging on the walls. It was empty, just like he'd left it, and it was just the way he needed it. But he could only be here when a priest wasn't. His decision to come now was a risk, but he was determined despite what may result.

Tentatively, he left and his fog oozed its way into the hall. It crept along the floor toward the bell tower door. It surrounded the door, seemingly undecided if it should enter. He felt a strong urge to visit all his cherished places, but he knew of another place much more important, and time was no doubt quickly running out.

Unable to resist, the door suddenly blasted open and the fog was sucked in. Daniel swirled himself around the rounded walls, spiraling up toward the bell. At the top, the bell started to chime. He looked outside at the neighborhood—his neighborhood, and his devastation. He basked in a moment of satisfaction, but realized he still had a job to do if it was to remain this way. He looked back into the dark tower below then dove straight down toward the door.

He rushed out from the room and continued thunderously toward the stairs. Enough with the tour and the teasing, he thought. His storm whistled in the narrow hallway as the bell chimed erratically. The fog quickly filled the stairwell and funneled into the foyer.

Daniel gathered himself but stayed vaporized as he stared at the gothic, double doors. He knew all too well what the room beyond them represented. When others were in control, he was weak here. Its walls were silent to him. He felt abandoned and deprived of the greatness he had been sent here to achieve. When he controlled it, it was his gateway to everything he represented. This was where he received his orders; his praise and punishment.

Although he cherished its very existence, he feared what would happen if he failed again. Grace's words had stung him. *What other plans have you got to impress the mightiest of all sinners?* He didn't have an answer to that, but he knew he needed this place if he was going to succeed. He moved forward slowly and gently seeped through the cracks of the doors that sealed his temple.

He gathered himself again and hovered just beyond the doors. He took time to look at the pristine cathedral laid out in front of him. At first, it was almost too much for his eyes to take. He'd seen it like this before when he came with Jada, but he could never get used to seeing his palace in this state. He wanted to wreak havoc on these walls, just as he had encouraged the kids to do in the past. When this place had been his, he needed that destruction to operate here. It had to be in ruin. It had to represent the message he was always eager to relay. But now, it was obvious he had no control of it. Its beauty told the story of everything he despised. Someone else controlled it, but just like all the times before, sin would guarantee this would soon be his again.

He flew down the aisle. He engulfed the altar and sanctuary. Soon, his spirit of hell filled the room as Daniel, once again, existed in this great source of power. He knew his presence was not enough, though. In fact, he felt an existence much stronger than himself here. It was hard for Daniel to believe that was possible. It was there all around him, and he knew why. The priest still stood in his way, but he was also aware of another obstruction.

This was the true source of his current dilemma and all those from the past. He had always thought that tarnishing the reputation of priests would be enough, and it had been, but there had never been a lasting effect. Something had always gotten in the way of Daniel's plans. Just when everything had begun to line up, a new priest would appear and take it all away. It was happening again, and as he looked Christianity straight in the eye, he knew how weak he was not to have successfully done anything about it. He felt the time had come to deal with this higher power. The priest would have to go, but now he decided to deal with his mentor first.

The organ blasted with dark, depressing, devil music. It motivated him. He became enraged and sent his storm into the highest beams and below the lowest pews. Nothing moved from his assault, though. No windows broke. No wood cracked. The church was strong, and he knew it would become more solid the longer he let this go on. After a further moment of indulgence, the music calmed as did Daniel. He settled on the seat in front of the organ. He continued to play, entertaining himself, while he waited.

CHAPTER 39

FATHER BURKE WALKED SLOWLY along the sidewalk in front of the church. His cane assisted every step, but he didn't appear concerned about the handicap that plagued his old, frail body. He had been in this condition for quite some time. To be completely honest, he couldn't remember himself any other way. He was delighted by the moment—the crisp morning; the bright sun rising over the bell tower; the sound of the perfectly restored organ that filled the air.

He stopped and took a deep breath. He remembered what this place had been like just a short time ago. He thought of his concern about bringing Marcus back here. He hadn't been sure if it was the right move, but he could see now he couldn't have made a better choice. Marcus had been one of the few success stories who made it away from this neighborhood in one piece. It seemed wrong to have him come back, but St. Paul's was a great opportunity. It had been a surprise actually to Father Burke when Marcus accepted the offer of the church, but Marcus's past required forgiving. His work here showed his desire for redemption, and his future would most definitely reap great benefits for all those willing to receive them.

He started moving again, but as he got closer, he became concerned. Not for Marcus, his past, or his future. He had thought Marcus was in there playing the organ, but he suddenly realized Marcus couldn't play. Marcus had told him that, when he first visited the church. *Are you ready to play*, he remembered saying to Marcus. Marcus replied, *I don't know how.*

The music at first was welcoming and pleasant to Father Burke, but now it clearly was not what would be expected from a Christian church. This type of music could only be enjoyed by one person, he thought. The fact that it changed so suddenly made Father Burke realize that the intruder knew he was here.

A moment of anxiety shot through his body with that realization, but it didn't last long. He was actually surprised this was the first time the church had been violated since Marcus rebuilt it. He had worried the workers would only get half done before they abandoned the job fearing for their lives.

Before Marcus arrived, Father Burke struggled to keep the church intact. His failure had resulted in a disaster, and he considered destroying it completely—burning it to the ground, but while that would remove the bad that came from it, the good would also suffer. With the overwhelming feeling that good would prevail, he continued throughout the years to fight evil and deal with it the best he could.

He knew this visit would occur, though, but he didn't know to what extent the intentions would be. In the past, they had been horrific and pleasant—tragic and harmless. Regardless of what was about to happen, Father Burke knew no good would come from it. He thought Marcus was the target, and possibly with great will and determination, his frail body could deflect the attention away from him.

He had tried this in the past but was always unsuccessful. In fact, his efforts had backfired, and father Burke had become the main source of the harm that resulted. He sighed at the thought of that. He knew he couldn't let that happen again. He was prepared to do anything to ensure it wouldn't. He had brought Marcus here knowing this threat existed, so he felt indebted to protect him against it. Worse than that, he had kept it from Marcus. Marcus had come here blind, but this threat surely had its eyes wide open. Its intent was harm, so Father Burke had to be sure Marcus was sheltered from its existence.

***

FATHER BURKE entered the church from a side aisle. He knew this building better than anyone. He knew the entrances; the hidden passages, but he was fully aware that wouldn't do him any good in this case. All he could hope to gain from it was some form of temporary hiding place. He knew his presence was no secret, outside as well as in here now, but he was not prepared to give up his location yet. When eventually discovered, he wouldn't be able to move fast enough to flee if he had to. His entry into this church was a commitment he'd have to stick to regardless of this visit's result.

Just as he suspected, the intruder was an extremely unpleasant sight. Up until now, he had hoped his suspicions were wrong, and the beautiful day he'd enjoyed outside would remain that way; but that shimmer of light was suddenly snuffed out. It seemed his instincts today were dead on, and nothing could have been more of a disappointment to him.

He remembered well the last time he was face to face with this hideous creature, and the time before that, and before that. This no doubt would be another in the long list of confrontations as he watched Daniel sitting at the organ, playing softly with his back turned.

Suddenly, the bell in the tower began to ring. Light that had been shining through the stained glass faded. Father Burke looked up concerned that the beams would start shaking any moment. He knew of Daniel's capabilities. He also knew the restored church wasn't something Daniel would be fond of. Father Burke slowly made his way down the aisle. He decided there was no use delaying. This confrontation was inevitable, so he might as well get on with it.

Daniel turned away from the keys, but the music continued. Father Burke stopped. He held his cane out in front of him as though he was about to lecture a school child. "An active church of Jesus Christ will never allow the presence of Satan," he scolded.

"That's extremely kind of you to refer to me as Satan." Daniel got up and walked arrogantly in front of the altar. The music stopped. The bell stopped. He turned sharply. "Your priest is a sinner," Daniel snarled.

"The priest's sins can be redeemed by God, but the sins of a Satanist burn a soul forever."

"Well, that makes me look forward to forever. But what have you got to look forward to, old man? Surely you must be planning your demise." Daniel turned away and opened his arms to the elegance of the church. "And with that will come the end of your persistent annoyance that I've put up with for so many years." He sat down in a pew. "But, I have to ask about your new priest first. He's better than the rest. Why?"

Father Burke gave him no response. It was interesting to him, however, that Daniel felt this way about Marcus. He felt the same, but he could never put his finger on why. Sure, he had reasons for bringing Marcus here. He thought his youth and vibrancy would do only good things, but Father Burke knew Marcus was different. He saw it in him as a boy and at the seminary. Then here, his passion rose higher than any other priest who presided within these walls. It was a quality Father Burke admired because it represented a stronger faith than he even had himself.

Daniel took a bible from the rack in front of him. "And why is it that you could never accept what was supposed to be yours?"

Father Burke looked down and closed his eyes. The truth hurt even if it came from the man he least respected. "Because what was destined for the first son, the first son despised." He looked up, determined to defend his legacy. "An attitude gifted from our mother before she was savagely murdered during the birth of a devil child."

Daniel got up and turned around with extreme pride, like the winner of a game he had never lost. "Yes, I remember that. He dropped the bible. "It was a great beginning, wasn't it?"

"It was a beginning that should have ended right there, but now it's too late for that."

"Yes, much too late," Daniel said while nodding with a certainty that he was in full control.

Wind began to howl from behind the sanctuary. It quickly filled the church making it hard for Father Burke to stand. He used his cane for support while the organ pipes rattled, and the beams above him shook as he suspected they eventually would.

"But not for you," Daniel continued. "And when you're corpse becomes a feast for beetles and maggots, this place will be mine."

Father Burke's cane flew from his hand, forcing him to grab on to a pew. He knew he was no match for Daniel.

There had been a time when he could stand up to him, but over the years, Daniel had only become stronger while Father Burke grew weak. If he was going to make any difference right here—right now, it would have to be fast, decisive, and final.

Daniel continued, "No longer a church of Christ, but a Palace of Satan, making the failure of all good the door opener to my evil, lustful power. And of course, that door will bring domination for—" He began to grow like an animated tree, quickly filling the space with his overwhelming presence.

"But without it, you're a failure—again," Father Burke interrupted. "Just as you've failed to disgrace the priest, and in your domination ploys at the turn of the century and a decade later." Father Burke stood up to Daniel. "Does our father—your almighty Satan—really enjoy watching you fail? Wasn't your control over this church and exposing all the priest's sins intended to impress him?" He waited for a reaction. "I think your fire in his eyes has fizzled out."

A devilish laugh filled the cathedral. "Don't kid yourself. My plan is all he needs for faith. Something he can count on from at least one of his boys."

"And the other, as you say, is nearly dead." Father Burke fought through the wind. Without the use of his cane, he barely made it to the display of Vigil Lights farther down the aisle. He struggled to remove his robe then draped it over the lights.

"Go ahead, cover your blessed lights. They mean nothing

to me." Daniel said with an echoing laugh.

"They will. This is just the beginning of what was originally meant to be," Father Burke replied. He took his robe from the candle lit display as if ripping the sheets off a bed. He threw it into the wind. The robe burst into flames and flew toward the Sanctuary before settling on the altar below Daniel.

He watched the fire scorch Daniel and spread quickly, soon becoming an inferno even Daniel couldn't control. "Your animated greatness is nothing against the flame of Christ," Father Burke yelled above the howling wind and crackling flame.

He took a step forward, but he didn't have his cane anymore. He fell to his knees. He looked back, up the aisle. He saw his cane stuck in the shattered stained glass showing the birth of Jesus. He began to panic realizing he wouldn't be able to make it out of here. He tried to calm himself—convince himself this was necessary. Marcus could carry on with his lifelong desire to bring good here. He thought about Marcus's father and how he tried to get him to do the same thing. He remembered how terribly wrong that went.

As the fire grew, he sheltered himself beside a pew. He stayed low to avoid smoke that quickly surrounded him like a pack of wolves eying their prey. His eyes stung. He coughed uncontrollably. He started shaking, realizing what was about to happen.

He had never imagined himself dying from fire. He had always figured he was old enough to go in his sleep. But now, dying peacefully was out of the question. He was about to experience a painful death. He would feel the flame when it first touched him. He would inevitably try to get away from it, but it would soon overcome him. His clothes would protect him but only for a short time. Then, the fire would scorch his skin, and he would suffer and melt until he lost consciousness. He closed his eyes knowing he was not ready for that. Death was not the problem. Anticipating it was already killing him, though.

He looked back to the altar where he saw Daniel struggling with the unexpected flame. He knew it would do nothing to him physically, but the church… A small smile softened Father Burke's face as he watched.

CHAPTER 40

IT WASN'T A PARTICULARLY JOYOUS GROUP of commuters Marcus walked among after exiting the subway, but it was his first realization that Christmas season was here. People around seemed to be carrying more shopping bags than he'd seen any other time he'd been here. The dead giveaway was a man in a Santa hat trying to get his attention by shaking an empty donation pail. But Marcus didn't pay much attention to any of what went on around him. His head was consumed with all the terrible events happening, leaving Christmas the farthest thing from his mind.

There had been no sign of Louie since the encounter. Marcus had even tried to contact him with the cell phone Angelica had given him, but he gave up not knowing how to use that stupid thing.

At first, Marcus didn't feel like he could leave Jada alone, but Angelica convinced him that she still had the upper hand.

He knew she certainly had the ability for that from how she had handled the two of them in the past. She didn't have an iron fist, but her Italian, no-nonsense attitude sent a clear message when she wanted it to be heard. The fact that Louie hadn't come back made Marcus believe this had not changed. Reluctantly, though, he decided to go back to the church.

He was fortunate to have Father Burke take over because of his *personal issues*, as Father Burke so lightly referred to them. He had thought the Bishop would have a problem with his lack of commitment lately, but the opposite was the case. He was there every time Marcus needed him, and lately that was more often than not.

Marcus figured that having the church operating again was something Father Burke needed toward the end of his life, and he would do whatever he could to keep that in place. Marcus also knew his constant presence was needed there for more reasons than keeping the doors open. He thought it would help if he just focused his attention on one thing. The church was the best place for that, so he had left Jada with his mother and headed out on his own.

Right away his thoughts veered away from building up the church. The ride here had been filled with thoughts of Louie and Jada; a baby for Christ's sake. He wondered how much more things would have been messed up if he hadn't walked in on them when he had. He thought about Daniel; how he had successfully injected hate into every crack of this community, and how the church could defeat him given the time. If all that wasn't enough, there was a detective investigating the death of a kid he killed. He shook his head with overwhelming guilt and sin—the exact feeling he had been trying to get away from all along.

He continued along a common pathway and was shocked—broken out of his trance as a fire truck went screaming by. He thought it was nothing more than the reality of this broken neighborhood. The picture he had painted in his head about this place wouldn't have been the same without it. This depressed him even more, so he buried his head into his jacket and continued to trudge along, trying to think of nothing.

It was not until Marcus rounded the corner that he noticed all the commotion. Farther down the street was St. Paul's Catholic Church. His St. Paul's Catholic Church. His hard work; his dreams; his future… All of which was now in a blaze of fire that ironically lit up an otherwise depressed neighborhood.

Marcus stopped dead in his tracks and shook his head not willing to accept that he was actually looking at the church. He thought maybe he had taken the wrong street; the building burning was someone else's problem.

He looked at the barricades securing the area; the fire trucks that lined the street in front of the church. Crowds watched, but he noticed their interest didn't appear to be for the building. Some smiled as they watched the incredible flame. Others seemed overjoyed that they were the chosen ones who got to witness this. Marcus immediately thought they were more concerned about how they would describe this fantastic site to those who hadn't seen it.

He watched manned hoses pour streams of water as high as they could reach, like he was watching breaking news on midday TV. As he looked around, he realized what he saw was not some other place. He was suddenly terrified with the reality that he was exactly where he should be. He started running urgently toward the danger zone.

Marcus crashed through a barricade and attempted to approach the building. He had no concern for the fire. At this point, he barely even knew it crackled right in front of him. Quickly, he was held back by a fireman.

"Holy shit, man! Take a look," the fireman said.

"There's someone in there. The Bishop—" Marcus frantically looked around. "I know he is."

Marcus didn't even remember he was wearing his collar, but it was obvious that the fireman suddenly realized he was a priest. "As far as I know, Father, no one has come out, and this thing's been burnin' way too high for anyone to jump into it," the fireman said.

The fireman guided Marcus back behind the taped off area, insisting he go there despite Marcus's consistent objection. Marcus searched frantically for a way out of here. He had to get in the church somehow.

"He says there's someone inside," the fireman said to others close by. He turned away from Marcus. "Anyone see—"

The fireman's distraction gave Marcus an opening which he took in full stride. He reached the door and opened it wide. A funnel of wind sucked him in as if someone was over anxious to see him.

He landed, tumbling on the floor of the foyer. He recovered onto his knees then struggled to see through the thick smoke that filled the area. He looked back to see if any firemen followed him with intentions of dragging him back out of here. No one was there. The draft must have pushed them back leaving Marcus all alone.

He looked to the church doors. The foyer he was in now had only started to burn, but he could see from the smoke forcing its way through the cracks in the doors that the church was burning with no possible hope of recovery. Was Father Burke in there? He thought of the possibility that he might be in the basement. He could be anywhere. Maybe he wasn't even here at all.

"Father Bur—" he yelled then broke into a coughing fit. He stayed on the floor and crawled toward the doors. Despite trying otherwise, he convinced himself that Father Burke was nowhere else. Once at the doors, he hesitated opening them fearing what he certainly would see. He touched the handle cautiously and pulled his hand back quickly after realizing how hot it was. He covered his hand with his jacket sleeve and pulled back the door. Flame did not assault him, but what he saw might as well have punched him straight between the eyes.

At the top of the aisle, he stood before the church witnessing the destruction of beauty. It wasn't so much the work he had done that concerned him, it was the fact that this could never be restored again. A magnificent building was completely ruined.

He remembered the look on the faces of onlookers outside. They didn't care. He knew they didn't. It had been what struck him as odd before the realization sunk in that this was happening to the church. He wondered if he was the only one who cared. If it was so unimportant to them, why was it so important to him? After all, he was one of them. He had been just like them, but for some reason he seemed to be the only one who changed. He began to walk down the aisle despite the imminent danger surrounding him.

Tears smeared the soot on his face while water fell in sporadic showers from the opened ceiling. A piece dropped behind the altar and crashed in a blaze of flame and ash. Another piece fell into the pews beside him. He threw himself away from it, falling into the aisle.

He got up cautiously and continued pushing forward. "Father Burke," he yelled again. The name echoed among the fiery crackle of flames. Another beam fell. He ducked. He called again, weakly, "Father…"

An echo responded, "Marcus, Marcus, Marcus."

The bell began to ring followed by the soft sound of the pipe organ. A peaceful choir joined in. This struck Marcus as odd. Where would choir music be coming from in the middle of this inferno? He could only see it as the beginning of the end for him. He realized he was now surrounded in flame. "Dear, God, with your help—" he said quietly to himself.

A noise—movement came from the side aisle. Marcus

looked up with a shimmer of hope, but he was distracted. The choir faded as well as the organ. The bell got louder, and rang in unison—like a countdown to death. Each ring was louder than the last. The tenth ring was deafening to him. Then there was the sound of destruction as though something was coming down.

Suddenly, behind the altar, the bell tower crashed through the wall. The bell clanged with thunderous impact and the organ started again. This time the music wasn't pleasant. Neither was the choir that joined in with the screaming, scratching, barking sounds of a black metal band.

If this was the end for Marcus, he felt like he was about to meet his maker. There was a price to pay for all he had done, and Marcus truly believed God had just denied his admission.

When the dust, ash, and flame settled, Daniel stood in front of the altar. His clothes were burnt. His face and hair were scorched but otherwise, he was unaffected by the surrounding blaze. "Sad, isn't it? Such a great man perishing so tragically," he said. He looked to the floor in front of the first pew. "And he didn't even realize that burning this place down would only be disastrous for you." Daniel looked back to Marcus. "How will you ever recover?" He slammed Marcus with a hideous smile.

Marcus tried to move toward what Daniel had been looking at, but a huge swell of fire held him back. He wasn't sure what Daniel was referring to, but something was there—someone. *Father Burke...* He turned away from the fire, and a force pushed him into the pews.

Daniel hovered over top of him when he recovered. Marcus rose without Daniel touching him. They came face to face.

"Now, my only concern is the baby," Daniel said. "Jada's baby. Your ultimate sin. Your bastard."

Marcus lunged at him, but instead of assaulting this hideous creature, he fell from the height, back into the pews.

Daniel laughed triumphantly at the weak attempt.

Marcus desperately scurried out from the pews and stumbled in the aisle, falling in front of the first pew. A beam fell next to him, crashing into the altar. A piece pined his leg as fire from the smashed altar burned violently.

Struggling to get free, he saw Daniel at the top of the main aisle looking down at him. Daniel backed up a few steps with an arrogant smile. The entrance to the church collapsed in flames before him. Marcus struggled to see beyond the debris, but he knew Daniel was no longer there.

Marcus turned to see Father Burke lying motionless at the end of the side aisle. Marcus fought to free himself from the beam then moved desperately toward him, falling at his side.

Father Burke coughed weakly and opened his eyes while Marcus held him. "I'm an old man, Marcus. Not worth risking your life for."

"If it weren't for you, I wouldn't have had this for a second chance." Marcus looked up for a way out.

"Your father said the same thing to me a long time ago."

This startled Marcus. *Why would Father Burke talk about my father at a time like this?* He responded, "My father?"

"He was a good man."

Marcus saw that the aisle was blocked with burning debris, but in front of the first pew, there was a clear path to a side door.

"You're a lot like him, son."

With renewed strength, he took Father Burke into his arms and began a serge toward the door.

"His passion for this church."

Marcus made it past the center aisle.

"His commitment. His desire."

Suddenly, pipes from the organ fell.

"His love of life."

Without hesitation, Marcus jumped onto a burning pew while fire burned wildly at his feet. He leaped back onto the floor and crashed into the door with his shoulder, smashing it wide open.

Outside, Marcus rolled on the ground, dropping Father Burke on impact. He crawled to Father Burke's side. Father Burke looked at him as though none of what just happened, had.

"Then, I took it from him," Father Burke said.

Marcus looked at him with confusion. "Took what? My father took his own life." Marcus had been told his father was troubled and was unable to handle the pressures that surrounded him. His mother had told him that. Father Burke had told him the same. *Now, what are you saying? He committed suicide, dammit!*

"All because of one man." Father Burke paused with a

look of extreme concern. "Be damned, the soul of the devil."

Father Burke took Marcus's hand in desperation. Fear overwhelmed his face as though his time was cursed. "Forgive me, Father." He blinked. He struggled for a short gasp of air. "For I have—" He blinked weakly. A blank stare was all he had left.

Father Burke was dead.

CHAPTER 41

JADA LOOKED AROUND THE ROOM that used to be Marcus's but was now occupied by her. She sat on the edge of the bed folding her clothes slowly. She thought that not having a room was a good reason for Marcus leaving, but really he'd probably left because of all the shit she'd gotten him into. Certainly, getting far away from her was all he had thought about since she'd been here. It would be his only option if he was going to stand any chance getting himself out of all this.

Up until now, she wouldn't have cared at all about that, but something had suddenly changed in her. She touched her stomach. She sighed and rubbed the side of her face with the other hand. She got up and took a small pile of clothes to a chair by the window.

She wondered if she should even still be here. Marcus and Angelica instantly sided with her over Louie, and why wouldn't they? She had their sympathetic vote, but that didn't mean she had any right to Marcus's bed. She'd come here with bad intentions for this family, and now she felt like she was part of it. Louie was the outcast, and it was like she replaced him. It must have been that sudden change in her that let her see what was terribly wrong with that.

Her chance with Louie Castellani had come and gone. Since he was still alive, it looked like she'd blown what she had planned through his brother. She doubted if she could have pulled it off anyway. Thinking about killing Louie Castellani—planning it; getting right down to the actual moment was a whole lot different than plunging the knife, twisting the blade, and watching blood drip from it afterward.

She wondered what would have happened if Marcus hadn't come when he did. She doubted Louie would have second guessed her death, so the outcome probably wouldn't have worked in her favor. Maybe that would have been better. At least then she would be with Seth.

She shook away that thought not really knowing what she truly believed. She looked around the room and realized that by being here, she was losing her independence. She was a street kid, and she thought she had been a pretty damn good one. But now, she was being taken care of by a lovely, caring, Italian woman and her son, who just happened to be a priest. *Just how the hell did I end up here?*

The window was right beside her. It made her think—stay or leave? Her desire was to stay, but she knew she should leave. She'd done her thing, and now it was time to figure out how to move on.

Marcus was the man who caused her to be like this, but he wasn't going to be a father to this child. She knew that. The longer she stayed, the harder that realization would be for both of them.

The only thing really keeping her here was the prospect of a doctor's appointment Angelica had set up for her. To Jada, this would be the real thing, not like what she would get on her own. A teenage pregnancy hotline would push her off to a free walk-in clinic. That wasn't all that appealing to her since their only intention would be to prevent her from sucking this thing out with some homemade abortion technique.

Outside, she saw Angelica's manicured backyard, stripped of its beauty because of winter approaching. She stepped away from the window and saw herself in a full length mirror on the closet door. She looked at her face, and it looked more stressed now than when she had seen herself in public washrooms just a short time ago. She followed her body down and stopped at her stomach. Her worried expression was now justified with a pregnancy that was a rapidly growing time bomb. That do it yourself solution she had just thought about was suddenly looking like her only option.

"Jada, I'll be out back for a bit," Angelica yelled from another room.

Jada didn't answer. She was still occupied with her dilemma, and her realization that she would have to continue on her own. She knew she should feel lucky to be here, but the reality of it all was, she lost her game of revenge for Seth and was left with this as her consolation prize.

CHAPTER 42

MARCUS WAS DEVASTATED. He watched a stretcher, with a covered body, being loaded into the back of the ambulance. The doors closed. He stood alone.

Everything suddenly seemed gone to him, like he would be starting from scratch if he managed to survive the troubles he still had to face. There would be no church left when the beams stopped smoking. His mentor would only be a memory he could think back on. His pride of becoming a priest was nothing but shame. He couldn't possibly imagine what he would do or where he would go from here.

Louie appeared beside him. He touched Marcus's arm to guide him away. "Sorry, man. Come on."

Marcus didn't move or look at him. "You been home?"

"No."

"You should go home. Ma worries about you." Marcus continued watching the ambulance crew take away Father

Burke's body. If he had nothing else, he still had Louie and his mother. Keeping them together became paramount. They had always been with each other which was much more than he had to offer either of them. "You should go home, Louie." Marcus watched for a moment longer.

An image of Daniel flashed in his eyes. "Who is that guy?"

"What? What guy?"

Marcus turned to him. "The old guy... From the parking lot."

Louie squinted his eyes. He appeared to look away, but he didn't.

"From the parking lot, Louie! Who is he? What's he want with Jada?"

"What do you want with her? She's a damn street kid, a goth chick, a fuckin' devil worshipper." Louie looked away for real, shaking his head. "What shit are you into, bro? He's their leader. A fuckin' full time freak."

"Father Burke talked about dad just before he died. Said he didn't kill himself. Said it was all because—"

Marcus started to leave quickly.

"Whoa. Where you goin'?"

"Home," Marcus said without turning back.

CHAPTER 43

AFTER PUSHING OPEN THE BACK DOOR, Angelica struggled with two bags of garbage. She sighed with relief when she got outside and looked into her backyard. It was fine to be taking care of Jada, she thought, but getting a moment to herself in her favorite place was wonderful relief. With winter coming, it didn't look like much out here, but she was well aware of all the work it required in the spring, summer, and fall. Seeing it ready for winter was, absolutely, just as rewarding.

She scanned the whole area until her eyes fell on disaster. She dropped the bags. He was far enough away for her to feel like she was just seeing things, but there was nothing imaginary about that face. She stood in shock as if a ghost from her past was about to make up for lost time.

Daniel leaned against a leafless tree near a fence that lined the back of the property. "Is this the tree you told the boys he hung himself from?" He gave her a look of arrogance and approval. "Ahhh. A dance with the devil to spare the young darlins."

Angelica was motionless and speechless. Events from years ago flashed in her mind: Her husband's work belt; him leaving with Marcus as a boy; watching him waving from high up in the bell tower; the look on Marcus's face when he found out his father was dead.

"It's been such a long time, Angelica, but you disappoint me. A corpse would show more glee."

"Please, leave me alone. You've taken enough from me already."

Daniel stepped away from the tree and slowly walked toward her. "That's not the way I remember it. I have no riches from your loss."

Nervously, Angelica attempted to go back into the house. She hadn't stepped away from the door, and he was the whole yard away. Regardless, she knew he was still too close. She turned back, but Daniel was immediately beside her now. He pushed the door shut.

"Or maybe I do. Marcus is very much like him, don't you think?"

She looked at him. He had a genuine, reflective look, but she could see deception right through it. She had hoped he'd moved on or died. She had simply tried to forget about Daniel from the past, but she realized now that her past never really went anywhere. The question was, how much of it was he going to expose?

"He was such a troubled man," Daniel continued.

Calmly, he put his hand on Angelica's back. She felt his push, leading her into the yard. She didn't resist, but she knew she should have. Jada was in the house. She could help. She was confused, however, about the past and what was happening. Oh God, she thought. Jada...

"What, with being controlled by Satan yet led by God. A confused life like that isn't really worth living, is it?"

He stopped her at a bush that now appeared lifeless. She looked at the bush only; not at him. She knew what he was talking about. She'd denied it all—to herself; to the boys. Until now, that all worked out fine, but she was suddenly terrified the blurred past was about to become perfectly clear.

"I guess that's what my brother thought. Imagine him and what was going through his mind?"

He turned her toward him, getting very close. She resisted, but he would have none of that. She didn't want to hear what she'd always suspected, but refused to accept. *Constantine killed himself.* That was all she needed to believe. That was all she needed to understand. That was all the boys needed to know.

Daniel continued, "Having to perform that Mass. The organ playing, the choir singing, all the God worshippers anticipating his sacred words."

He touched her face. He stroked it softly while he wiped a tear away.

"Knowing all along your husband hung from the rope that rang the last bell." He looked beyond her, dazed in reflection. "But, it was a great loss, Angelica. After all the time I spent recruiting my inside man. My brother... He saw right through my plans for Constantine, and not a second was wasted trying to win him back."

Angelica closed her eyes and turned away. "Condemning Constantine to Satan wasn't enough for you? What could you possibly want from me now?"

Daniel looked away, toward the house. "I'm proud of your boys, Angelica. They're both great sinners. Fine examples to carry on your family name."

"Just leave us alone." She truly hoped that he would leave. Surely, he didn't plan to go after Marcus and Louie the same as he did Constantine. *What if he already had?*

He turned back abruptly and pulled her close to him. "That, unfortunately, I cannot do. Again, I find myself drawn to your loving kindness just like so many cling to my selfish greed."

Shock and terror fill her face. *Was he here for her, again?* She saw him look back to the house and the window above. He pushed Angelica away like a piece of trash he had no use for anymore.

"And just as before, I'm not interested in sharing."

She saw Jada standing in the window and Daniel was fixated on her. Angelica was suddenly aware of Daniel's plot. *How would he know about Jada? How much did he know?* She ran desperately for the door. "Is there no limit to the innocence you're willing to corrupt?"

As she reached the door, the brute force of Daniel's iron fist slammed against the frame. She closed her eyes and sighed remembering clearly the anger he was capable of.

Angelica was thrown back and fell violently, sliding along the patio. She was unable to stop from rolling and came to an abrupt stop. She tried to get up immediately but wasn't able to get her feet under her body. She saw the yard spinning out of control. She expected Daniel to grab her, so she tried to protect herself. Nothing touched her, though. She remembered falling again after not being able to stand. There was a thud to the side of her head. Pain rushed through her body instantly. She saw the yard again, but this time it was sideways. The grass was blue and the sky green. Then, it all went black.

CHAPTER 44

MARCUS WAS PARTIALLY OUT OF LOUIE'S CAR as it squealed to a sudden stop in Angelica's driveway. He exited without bothering to close the door, and he led the way to the front door. He looked back to see if Louie was getting out. He was, but he was barely moving.

On the way over here, Marcus had pushed Louie to drive faster. Even Louie's pedal to the metal mentality wasn't enough speed. He told him more of what Father Burke had said about their father; how he thought Daniel was involved and probably their mother. Louie didn't seem convinced.

Marcus realized Louie was probably more concerned about coming back here and facing his own secrets. Eye contact with him now confirmed it. Jada would be here, his mother, and of course Marcus. He would be forced into an explanation about Jada and him which was something he obviously didn't want to get into. If Marcus was wrong about

Daniel, he could see why Louie wasn't right on his heels.

Marcus burst into the house. With or without Louie, it made no difference to him. He had a hunch something was terribly wrong. Hopefully, he wasn't too late. Marcus yelled, "Ma!" There was no answer. He moved quickly to the kitchen. "Ma! Ma! Jada!"

Nothing… There were no voices and no movements, other than what Marcus was making on his own. If they weren't here, where would they be? He remembered a doctor's appointment, but he was sure that wasn't today. In fact, he remembered Angelica on the phone, pushing the receptionist for an earlier date from someday next week.

He looked quickly into the living room before he moved to the hallway. There were no signs of any disturbances. No dishes were left on the table. The TV was off. He looked into his bedroom but didn't go in. He ran to Angelica's bedroom. "Ma!" he yelled again.

She wasn't there. From what he could tell, no one was in the house. The last time he saw Jada, she was in no shape to be going anywhere except to a doctor. That's why Angelica was so persistent with the receptionist. He should have never left, he thought. He had been worried about Louie returning, but he wasn't the problem now.

He turned back to his room. "Jada!" He knew he wouldn't find them there either. He stopped at the doorway breathing heavily. Maybe they got an appointment. *Yeah, that's it. Ma insisted, and they're with the doctor now…*

Louie yelled from outside, "Marcus! Marcus, get out here!"

Marcus ran to his bedroom window and saw Louie kneeling beside Angelica on the patio. His first instinct was to rush out there, but the world suddenly slowed down for him. He watched Louie actually caring for their mother. He didn't think Louie was capable of anything like this, especially after learning what he had done to Jada's boyfriend. He thought Louie was still living here because of how convenient it was for him. It was a great place for him to get away from street life, and where better could he dig himself into a hole when he needed to. But watching him with Angelica made him realize that Louie was still here to take care of her. His father was gone. Marcus had found another path in life. If Louie had left, she'd be alone; he'd be the same as his older brother. But Louie was nothing like Marcus. Mostly, that was not good. In this case, Louie was the clear winner. Marcus watched them a little longer, but the moment quickly caught up and Angelica's crisis took over.

Outside, Marcus slid to his mother's side, knocking Louie out of the way. He immediately checked for a pulse. "Call an ambulance! Shit, man, get some help here."

Louie was already on his cell phone.

Marcus had instantly figured out what happened here. Jada was gone; he knew that, and it was Daniel who took her. His mother and father; Father Burke and Daniel... They all had a past together that resulted in his father's death, and it was Father Burke who did it. He couldn't imagine that, but Father Burke had said it himself. Even if Father Burke caused his death, however, it had been no doubt orchestrated by

Daniel—the same man who had Jada. The same man who had his unborn child.

Angelica opened her eyes and smiled. At that moment, she seemed okay to Marcus. Her eyes were warm and caring. She smiled at him just as she always had. She didn't say anything. She didn't even try to. She seemed peaceful, now that her two boys were with her. He looked beyond her face and noticed her body was trembling. She tried to move her arm to Marcus, but she couldn't. Her eyes closed.

CHAPTER 45

MARCUS PACED IN A WAITING ROOM while Louie stood at the reception desk that was sparsely littered with Christmas decorations. He watched Louie filling out a form with more papers sprawled out in front of him. He noticed they were the only two there. He continued pacing and saw an excuse for a Christmas tree with no presents under it. He remembered how Angelica refused to give up on Christmas. Even when everyone else seemed to have lost faith in the season, she had been trying to revive it. He thought when he got back to the church he would do the same. *When I get back... What church?*

Until now, he hadn't thought about what happened at the church. *Father Burke... My god...* He remembered Daniel. It was like a dream now, but he knew Daniel was there. *Is it possible I imagined it all, and Ma just slipped and fell?* That seemed more realistic, but he couldn't convince himself. The church was burnt to the ground; Father Burke was dead; his mother was in serious condition; Jada was gone. *All because of one man... Be damned, the soul of the devil...*

As far as Marcus was aware, Louie didn't seem to really know who Daniel was. He knew Jada did, though, and probably Grace. Just then he realized he hadn't seen Grace in a while. She seemed to have lost touch with Jada ever since Jada had been staying at his place. She would probably know a lot. She might even know what was up with the detective who Marcus knew could be a real problem for him. He couldn't believe he had almost forgot about the kid he killed. He shook his head realizing his problems were stacking up so fast, he struggled to keep track of them all.

Now, his problem was his mother. She had somehow been dragged into all of this. Marcus racked his brain trying to figure out how that could be. Those thoughts took him back to his father and all the time they had spent together at the church. But Angelica never came. They must have all gone as a family at one point, but Marcus couldn't remember that far back. Then something must have happened... Whatever it was, it no doubt had something to do with Daniel.

Just then, Marcus noticed a doctor walk into the room. Marcus turned sharply.

The doctor asked, "Father?"

"She's okay, right? Tell me she's okay," Marcus said.

The Doctor shook his head. "She's not okay, Father. She's had a heart attack for one."

Marcus was shocked—defeated. This was his fault, he thought. He saw the look on the doctor's face. It said the same thing.

"Now that she's here, we can deal with that," the doctor continued.

Louie was suddenly right beside Marcus. "What was that? She's had what?"

"She's also in shock and not responding. I'm worried she won't come out of that." The doctor looked at them both curiously. "She may not want to for some reason."

Marcus noticed Louie was confused. He looked more worried than Marcus had ever seen him before. The doctor's accusation was obviously pointed directly at the two of them. Louie didn't seem to catch on, but Marcus did. The doctor's glare was a direct shot right between Marcus's eyes.

To Marcus, the doctor was searching for answers. He just hadn't said anything direct yet. Marcus thought questions were about to start. One would lead to another, and before he would know it...

"Have you been looked after, Father?"

That caught Marcus by surprise. He must have looked terrible, he suddenly thought. He looked down at his torn jacket that was covered in soot. He smelt like fire. Word of the church probably made its way here by now. If the doctor hadn't figured out it was his church, he would soon. That would no doubt start a question session. First from the doctor, then by the cops when they got here. He thought his only way out of this would be to leave, now, but how could he abandon his mother at a time like this?

Marcus turned away. "I'm fine."

Louie was still there ready to ask a question, but the words weren't coming out. Marcus looked at a door that would get him out of here. He thought Louie could handle this—he would have to... He continued toward the door then started running.

CHAPTER 46

MARCUS BURST OUT from the hospital's entrance and ran straight across the street into a park. He felt like he should keep running—just go somewhere and hide. Was that the only choice he had left—leave all of this behind and find somewhere else for a fresh start, again?

He had tried so hard to solve other people's problems. Now all those problems were somehow his. All he really wanted to do was make this place better than the disaster it had become. Now he was no longer the promising solution for everyone to look forward too, he was just another product of it all once again. He couldn't think of a better solution than to just leave. Despite that, he started to slow down then realized he was not alone. He turned quick to see Louie holding his pace.

Louie grabbed his shoulder and turned him around aggressively. "Who the fuck are you to wrap her up in some little street urchin's bullshit?"

Marcus pushed back. "How are you any different? In fact you're worse, feeding off them like a blood sucker."

"Fuck you, man. Our mother's up there dying because of you. Has God got you so wrapped up in yourself you can't even see that?" Louie backed away. "He doesn't give you that much power, Father. Your halo isn't that bright."

"You don't know shit, Louie." Marcus held his head with one hand. He scratched his eye. "As a matter of fact, neither do I." He turned away and walked to a bench nearby. He sat down without any fight left.

"Where is she, Marcus? After nearly taking Ma's life, what else did she take?"

"The way Ma is now has nothing to do with Jada, Louie."

"Fuck, man! Wake up. How could you possibly say that?"

"I told you in the car. This all goes way back, before Dad died."

Marcus thought about what more he should say to Louie. He could tell him everything right here—right now. He shook his head and held his fist to his mouth. *But how am I going to get those words to come out?*

"Just go back, Louie. You can handle it. You've been taking care of her for all this time." He looked at Louie with pleading eyes. "I left you all alone before without a plan, and you did fine. I'm not sure how, and I don't want to know anymore than I already do; but I know you and Ma were better off without me, so just go and do what you've been doing."

"Seriously? You come back all poised on your throne and high church, and now you just toss in your robe thing, and tell the street thug to carry on?" Louie sighed. "I know what I am, Marcus. Unfortunately, it's all I know. I have to do the things I do to stay alive. It's simply the way things are. But you were supposed to change that. What happened to that plan?"

Marcus was shocked hearing that coming from Louie. He couldn't believe Louie had actually thought about what he came back for. He thought Louie had always seen his older brother as a joke. He had never really listened to him when they were kids, and now the priest thing had likely put him over the top. But that wasn't what he just said. He was looking to Marcus for help. He probably always had…

Marcus suddenly wondered how much Louie knew about what had happened. He held back from talking but finally said, "After Dad died, I was just like you. I was bent out on everything. I lied, cheated, stole. You were too young to realize." He paused with a deep breath. *That was likely my first mistake. You probably knew exactly what was going on.* "When mom told me years later he had killed himself, I got my wakeup call—my calling, so I became a priest."

He watched Louie step toward him—a step forward, not a step back… Louie didn't shake him off. He was embracing his older brother as one of his own. Marcus had been concerned that if Louie knew all about Daniel, his reaction would be nuclear. Now he didn't think that. Louie would never take anything sitting down, but there was a reason why he'd survived this long doing what he did on the streets. Marcus was suddenly convinced that telling Louie everything wouldn't hurt at all.

At this point, if he didn't tell Louie, he would be alone to figure this out. He couldn't leave, he had a baby to worry about and a detective… Louie was the only chance he had. Better than anyone he knew here, Louie would know what to do. At the very least, he would jump right in, fists ready.

"You want to know why Jada?" *Brace yourself, bro. This is gonna shake your world.* "The baby's mine." He paused and considered his next sentence. "And I killed a kid to get her away from that bastard."

He watched Louie for his reaction. For Louie, this was nothing unusual, and his response showed exactly that. Marcus was surprised, but he shouldn't have expected anything else. Considering who Louie was now, this must be everyday business, he thought. It was unusual to watch this coming from his younger brother, though. Instead of freaking out; instead of him busting into a cover-up scheme, Louie calmly sat down beside him—a true street pro. There was no doubt about that.

Marcus continued, "I watched him with all that control he has over those kids. I craved his power. I envied him and despised him at the same time."

He looked to Louie who was just listening. He must have been thinking that his brother hadn't changed much. Louie simply reacted when things went wrong, and he was now hearing that his older brother was exactly the same.

"And worst of all, I was too proud to admit any of it. I preach others to redeem themselves—to confess their sins, but I'm too proud to do it myself."

"Does that make you a bad priest? The way I see it, it makes you human," Louie said.

"Louie, we have to be able to see our mistakes. I've been taught that confessing them cleanses your soul. But all the teaching never showed me how to do it myself."

"You just did, but I doubt I'm gonna have much pull."

Marcus shook his head. "No, Louie, you're wrong. You're my brother. No one could be better."

Louie laughed that off. "Your choices suck."

"I left here because this place sucks. I came back to make a difference, expecting my change to lead the way. But change only leads the truly faithful, and we both know there's no one truly faithful around here."

He watched Louie reach into his pocket and take something out. He passed Marcus's missing crucifix. "I meant to give it back," he said.

Marcus looked at it. *But you didn't, and you didn't throw it away either.* Beneath all the toughness and lack of faith he showed, Louie believed in something. Marcus knew that now. He had always wanted to teach Louie that, but the words never got through. At least he thought they didn't. *Just how much of me is in you, Louie? Is it possible if I hadn't gone away, you wouldn't have ended up the way you did?*

Marcus reached for the crucifix but only touched it. He looked straight into Louie's eyes. "It was Dad's. Did you know that? Ma gave it to me at my ordination."

"Damn," Louie said. "I never got nothin' like that."

The smile on Louie's face let Marcus know he meant nothing by that. "It's helped me get this far. Now, my faith can take over," Marcus said then nodded to Louie. "Change, brother." He closed Louie's hand without taking the crucifix. "You're running out of time." *And trust me, there's no worse feeling.*

Marcus looked at him with love only two brothers knew. He felt so much better having told Louie about his sins. An extremely dark cloud had been lifted, leaving his path clear to redeem himself for what he had done. He didn't know how he would accomplish that, but he could now go about it without a guilty conscious. The guilt was still his, but Marcus knew God would help.

He knew his mother would want both of them with her, but she was in good care now. There was nothing he could do for her except sit and wait for the clouds to close back in.

He knew Jada was in great danger, though. Daniel no doubt had her. He would have killed her before if it hadn't been for Marcus.

He also knew Louie needed him, and he needed Louie...

"I have to save Jada and my baby," Marcus said.

CHAPTER 47

IT WAS THE SAME STREET Grace had always looked at when she stepped out from the small door that led to her apartment. It was the same bar across the street; the same parking lot farther down; the same alley… But something about all of this wasn't the same at all. What had always been an entertainment zone at this time of night, now looked like a waiting area for a rehab clinic. The bar was open and plenty of people were around to fill it, but they were not going there. Its usual customers were nowhere in sight. The only people in the area were goth kids—hundreds of them.

She stepped onto the sidewalk and was immediately blocked by more crime scene tape that sectioned off part of the sidewalk and the alley. She took a quick look into the alley when she passed by. She saw the fire escape that usually took her to and from her apartment. The garbage bin Daniel had been staked out beside was there. She could still make out

Detective Monroe's bloodstain marking the asphalt like grease on a carpet or the scars on Daniel's face.

After she had gotten away from Daniel during her desperate escape, she had the taxi driver circle around to see if Daniel was still there. At first he had refused, but eventually his curiosity got the best of him. Just as she had suspected, Daniel was nowhere to be seen. She had the taxi driver drop her off farther down the street. From there, she'd snuck back to the door she had just come out of. When she had gotten safely back in her apartment, she'd looked out her window and into the alley. The body was still there.

When the detective's discovery was made at daylight, Grace had been the first to be questioned. She remembered her fear of getting caught right then. Her only alibi was as obvious as her faked bedtime eyes. *I was sleeping. I didn't hear a thing.* Remarkably, that was good enough for the new detective on the scene, and to this date, she hadn't heard another word about it.

She stopped when she completely passed the alley to get a better feel for what she had come out here for. She watched the gathering going on in front of her. She had seen it happening from her apartment but only slightly. Enough, though, to know something was off, and she needed to find out what was going on.

She thought the right kids would tell her. Often, however, when things like this happened, no one knew anything. They all just reacted to each other with no real meaning or purpose. She watched them walk slowly along the sidewalk on both sides of the street. They loitered in groups on the corners and in doorways. From what she could see, it was just a gathering at this point. If it had anything to do with Jada, which Grace suspected it did, information would certainly be hard to come by.

Grace knew Marcus had taken her to his mother's house. She also knew no one was there now. Even though Jada could have gone anywhere, she couldn't help but think the worst. This sudden gathering confirmed for her that Jada was with Daniel, and he had sent word out that the sinners would soon sin again. She feared for her and thought someone out here would know something. Even if she got some answers, what would she do, she thought? She didn't know.

Answers led to actions and actions to solutions. At least she knew that, and surely someone out here would start talking. She would only need confirmation from one person. With that she would begin searching for Jada. If she was still with Marcus, then she was fine, but she wasn't with him. Grace was sure of that from the sinking feeling in her stomach.

Standing in one spot wasn't going to do her any good, so Grace started moving. Throughout this odd looking environment, she moved quickly from group to group. She was not dressed like the others, but she had no problem fitting in. They all knew her. They greeted her, talked to her, and even showed affection toward her; but she didn't get what she was looking for, so she moved on.

Grace talked to another group then continued farther

down the sidewalk to a few kids walking. There was consensus among the bleak clothing and made up faces—no one knew where Jada was. At least that's what they all said. Maybe they really didn't, she thought. Maybe this was all about Daniel finding Jada and not some perverted celebration for him having her by his side again. If that was the case, she was no worse off than Daniel himself. She would just have to be sure she found Jada first.

She ran across the street. She was frustrated as she walked toward the bar. She wasn't exactly sure what was going on, but she had no intention of giving up until she did. She stopped and considered going back the way she had just come. She looked back across the street then moved on with uncertainty.

She realized she was alone now. For some reason, the kids were keeping their distance—like oil in water. If anyone should scurry from here, it should have been her. She really didn't belong out here among all these kids, and she could see everyone had begun to figure that out. The word of her looking for Jada had obviously spread quickly. Whatever this was about, it included Jada. She knew that for sure now, but she still didn't have any idea where Jada was.

Suddenly, she was grabbed from behind and swiftly forced down a side street.

Grace fought unsuccessfully as she was pushed across the street toward a car. She thrashed wildly to get free and see her attacker, but she was no match for him. She knew it was a guy, and she guessed it wasn't any of the kids. He had no trouble controlling her as he opened a car door and pushed her into the back seat. When he got in with her, she saw who he was. She knew that face. *Damn, Louie Castellani.*

She had thought all along that Daniel had Jada, and this goth gathering was set up by him. Jada's plan had been to get close to Louie Castellani, though. How much closer could she get than in the place he called home? How much time would it take him to discover her there? How much luck would she need to carry through with her revenge for Seth? Now that Grace knew Jada was unsuccessful, what was the chance she was still alive; and what the hell did Louie Castellani want with Grace?

When he shut the door, the car pulled away. Grace fought violently—kicking, punching, screaming; all of which Louie had no trouble controlling. He pushed her head back against the seat with his hand firmly against her mouth. He looked at her square in the eyes. "No biting, okay?"

She glared at him with her mouth full of his hand. He began to take it away, slowly.

"Go easy. One bite and your head will pay."

It must be about the money, she thought. He must have done the same to Jada as he had done to Seth, but he still had an issue with the money. "You fuckin' bastard. I've got nothing to do with your damn money. There's no fuckin' way you're gonna get it anyway," Grace said.

"Calm down, Grace."

Those words came from the driver. She hadn't even considered anyone else since she was in this car. She knew it was moving, but who was driving didn't enter her mind. As the car continued around a corner, she realized she knew that voice. The car stopped.

"Grace, it's okay. Calm down," Marcus said as he turned around.

She stopped fighting. She gulped while she considered her options. She had known Marcus was Louie's brother, but she had figured Marcus didn't have a clue about Louie's life on the street. Now she started to think Marcus was in on the money. Maybe Louie worked for Marcus. What better cover would there be than him being a priest? Marcus knew of her relationship with Jada, so now they were after her for the money. She looked out the window not knowing how to handle this. *I killed a cop for this guy, dammit!*

"We're looking for Jada. Where is she, Grace?"

Grace was shocked. She had convinced herself in the past few minutes that Jada was dead, and she would be next. Now she believed the opposite. There was nothing different about Marcus. He looked depressed and confused just like before. He certainly didn't look like he was going to kill anyone, and she thought he probably didn't even know about any money. She looked to Louie who didn't appear all that inspired with death either.

She looked back to Marcus. "She's supposed to be with you."

Marcus asked, "Why are all the kids in the street?"

She glanced back at Louie. "He's not gonna put a bullet in my head is he?"

"Why, you owe me somethin'?" Louie asked.

"He's my brother, Grace."

That doesn't mean he's not the asshole I've learned to hate. "He's lucky he's not dead." She turned to Marcus. "You know why she saved you don't you?"

"Grace, I don't care about that. I just have to find her."

"Well you should care about how your asshole for a brother steals, and cheats, and controls, and kills in these streets. You're a priest for Christ's sake. Why wouldn't you care about that?"

"Grace, she's carrying my baby. I need to find her."

She nodded and looked out the window. "Yeah, me too. All those bloody people out there, and no one knows nothin'. Fuckin' bullshit." She continued to look out at the darkness. "I know he's got her." She was at least relieved. She knew she wouldn't have to fight for her life—at least now she wouldn't—and she had someone to work with to find Jada. "Why am I the only one who wants to get her away from him?"

"Daniel's got them all."

She saw Marcus watching her through the reflection in the window. His caring eyes made him such a convincing priest.

He asked, "Why not you?"

She still looked out the window. "I heard the church is gone. It was my only hope."

"There are other churches, Grace." She noticed him wipe his eye. "By the way, you're not the only one."

She looked to Louie. *How am I going to do this—find Jada*

with Louie Castellani? She locked eyes with Marcus's reflection.

"He's my brother, Grace."

CHAPTER 48

IF THE UNDERGROUND BALLROOM wasn't ominous enough, now it was completely crawling with weirdness. Jada stood in darkness, probably unnoticeable to those she could see. She tried to adjust the red hood that blocked her vision, but someone right beside her made sure her hands stayed at her sides. Another hooded guard was poised on the other side of her. She was being held back here like a prized fighter, or in this case the underdog who had no idea about the battle ahead. She knew the guards were both there to be sure she stayed exactly where she was.

She saw many others, but none dared step beyond the pillars surrounding the room. That made it obvious that the main area was reserved for what was about to happen. This moment appeared to be a waiting period which Daniel would no doubt use to exercise his arrogance. She had already been there for quite some time. How much longer she had to wait would be just a guess. In his mind, he was a rock star, so any event he'd planned would go off on his schedule. Judging by the anticipated looks on the faces near her, though, no one was about to leave due to a no-show.

She figured this ceremony, or event, or whatever they called it was all because of her; but she wasn't sure if it was for reward or punishment. With Daniel, she could never tell, and she had no information that would lead her either way.

After looking out Marcus's bedroom window, everything was just a blurred memory for her. She wasn't sure how they drugged her; who did it or why, but she was fully conscious now. Her bet was that it had been Daniel himself. He had been the last person she saw before now, so it only made sense he wanted her this way.

Judging by the surroundings, she was left with the feeling that nothing good would happen to her. She anticipated that she was about to be rewarded, but that was simply wishful thinking. She felt nervous knowing otherwise. Even those guarding her seemed on edge. Silence only added to the anxiety she felt, and she was eager to get on with it no matter which way this ended.

The torturing silence was replaced with a low drone of conversation. Curious eyes were watching all around. Then quietly, out of sight, she heard a monotone chant.

"...of the Earth. God of this World."

She had never been part of any ceremonies Daniel performed in the past, but she had heard about them from others who said they had. They were only rumors, and back then she didn't believe them. It never made any difference anyway. Let those who wanted to appear larger than they were get the fame they were looking for, she had thought. Jada had never been there for the faith Daniel preached. For her, it was all about Seth. She had thought Daniel was on a warpath for Seth too, but now she realized Daniel only ever looked out for himself.

She noticed a group of five appear from one side of the ballroom. They were wearing black robes with hoods just like the one she wore except hers was all red. All of their faces were totally covered, and it became obvious that they were the source of the chanting.

"Hail, Satan, Lord of Darkness," they continued.

If it were any other time, she may have found this parade interesting. It was dark and depressing—just the way she liked things ever since Seth's death; but she realized right then that it didn't need to be that way, and she didn't really want it to be. Her life on the street took a drastic turn when Seth was taken from her, but it hadn't always been like that. She was happy at one point, and she had been trying to find a way to get that back.

She had Grace who tried so desperately to change her. She had accepted Grace's efforts but never acted on any of them. Grace took her off the street and talked about how she found a way to stay off them herself. Jada wanted to follow that example, but she simply refused to let go of her determination to get payback for Seth.

Now she was here with nothing to show for it. She slowly

moved both hands to her stomach—a weak attempt to protect the only thing she had left.

Another group appeared from the other side of the room. They were also chanting. As the two groups became the center of attention for everyone else, they got louder. Jada felt the tension rising. She closed her eyes with the paralyzing thought that this was her destiny.

The chant continued, "King of Hell. Ruler of the Earth. God of this World."

Both groups moved toward the middle of the room. Others joined in chanting. The two guarding her were no exception. She felt like she would be nudged or punched if she didn't too, but that demand never happened. She never said a thing.

"Hail, Satan, Lord of Darkness. King of Hell. Ruler of the Earth. God of this World."

Those words rang in her ears as it was almost deafening now. The two groups formed a circle in the middle of the room and continued. It was joined with pounding—an organized applause for what they all anticipated.

With the loud commotion continuing, one of Jada's guards nudged her forward. She was being led toward the circle. She felt like running, but she knew she had nowhere to go. Resistance was another option, but what good would it do? All the eyes in the room were on her now, so cooperation seemed to be her only choice.

Soon she found herself alone in the middle of the circle, in the middle of the room; in the middle of where she thought just might be hell. She took a deep breath and closed her eyes. Maybe when she opened them this would all be a dream. Certainly, even a street kid from an extremely broken family shouldn't find herself in a situation like this. The deafening chant quickly broke her out of that thought.

"Hail, Satan, Lord of Darkness. King of Hell. Ruler of the Earth. God of this World."

All the voices suddenly went silent as if being queued by an offset Stage Manager.

Quietly, the words were repeated again. "Hail, Satan, Lord of Darkness. King of Hell. Ruler of the Earth. God of this World." But this time it came from only one voice.

The ballroom was deathly quiet now. Jada looked around wildly to see what she had missed. It was too dark for her to make out anything specific. She could only see close faces staring at her. She continued searching and finally saw someone moving toward the circle from the darkest corner of the room.

She knew who it was and that he was coming toward her. She instinctively looked in all directions for an escape route, but she was locked in place like a prisoner in chains. When she looked back, Daniel stood outside the circle in a decorated, red cape.

She watched him look around the room. He smiled and nodded, pleased by what he saw. There were many followers and many sinners. He marveled at his devil worshippers, she thought. He raised his arms.

"Hail, Satan, Lord of Darkness. King of Hell. Ruler of the

Earth. God of this World."

His words shattered the silence. They echoed in the room. She could tell they electrified his eager followers.

He walked to the center of the circle and locked his eyes on Jada. She had no choice but to stare back. It seemed her time for a daring escape was over. Now she would have to play this out and hope she would come out alive. He ripped her hood off and stood back so everyone could see her.

"Jada." He walked around her. "Our precious, Jada."

He touched her face. She cringed. He ran his finger between her breasts. She thought he would disrobe her, but he didn't. He placed his hand on her stomach and looked to the crowd. Her first reaction was to knock his hand away, but someone behind her must have anticipated that. She was now unable to move either arm.

"Our precious Jada has been fucked by a priest."

He quickly grabbed her chin and showed her to the crowd. She resisted his aggression, but could not control his strength with her head alone. She grinded her teeth and snarled back at him. She felt wetness in her eyes and tasted the saltiness of her tears.

"Now she carries his baby—a gestation influenced by—"

He suddenly let go of her. He turned away as if depressed. She gasped for air and tried to free her arms. Since she was unable to, her only defense was to hiss and snarl at her attacker.

"My precious Jada carries the sins of a priest." He held this thought while looking at the ground.

He looked back to her then to the crowd. She had a sudden feeling that it was all over, but she knew better than that. Daniel had a plan, and this was just the introduction. What would happen next, when and where she had no clue. But she knew from his demeanor he was done for now. Hopefully the haze wouldn't set in like before, she thought. She needed to be alert so she could think of a way out of this.

"Spread the word of a Black Mass," Daniel said as he left the circle. He lifted his arms to the crowd. "Black Mass!"

She watched those around him suddenly rejoice.

"Black Mass! Black Mass!" Daniel continued.

The worshippers joined in a deafening chant, "BLACK MASS."

CHAPTER 49

FROM THE WINDOW of Grace's apartment, Marcus looked into the alley below and heard a dull roar from the goth kids still flooding the area. Even though the window was closed, he could easily make out what all the excitement was about.

"Black Mass," they chanted.

It had started when the three of them were trying to make their way here. The excitement among the kids had suddenly intensified, and it became clear that word about Daniel's plans had made it onto the street. A Black Mass could only amount to one thing. Jada was about to be celebrated. In the mind of Daniel, however, Marcus thought that would definitely result in the worst...

Marcus left the window and began pacing between Grace's kitchen and the small adjoining living room. He had the look of a crazed man without sleep. He knew fatigue was setting in, but his mind was clear and focused on one thing.

It made sense that Daniel was a Satanist. All the things Marcus had learnt about him pointed to Satanism—what he had seen and what the neighborhood had become. But how vast was his influence, and for how long had this been going on? Marcus shook his head unsure of those answers.

If he had always been out there, thriving on youth, his message must have been passed from generation to generation. That explained why the neighborhood was like this, but it didn't answer why Marcus hadn't been involved until now. He had spent years in these streets, but he had never seen the likes of Daniel. There was crime, and greed, and hate; but it wasn't satanic. As far as he could tell, Louie was the same. Louie was a thug and a gangster, but he wasn't a Satanist. It was like both of them had been somehow protected from it all.

Marcus realized now that his father hadn't been so lucky. His death had been no doubt influenced by Daniel. Father Burke had somehow been involved, and by the looks of it, his mother too. That realization stopped Marcus from pacing. He looked back to the window.

Now his unborn child was in the hands of Daniel, he thought. He had been unable to influence the events from the past, but Daniel's control over his child and Jada was something Marcus simply had to stop.

He looked away from the window to see Grace pouring two cups of coffee at the counter that was littered with dried up dirty dishes. She turned to see him watching her.

"This isn't what you need," she said.

She handed him a cup, then he looked at Louie sleeping on the couch. He thought that if Louie could sleep through this, maybe he wasn't so innocent. Or maybe that was Louie as he'd always been. He just didn't give a shit.

"You're telling me we're over top of them right now?" Marcus took a drink. He knew the alley outside was where he and Jada had escaped into. The tunnel had led them there. Beyond the tunnel was the room. This Black Mass would definitely be conducted in that room.

"Rent's cheap," Grace said.

Marcus had to get back in there. He thought Grace must know another way in. He became suddenly frustrated with wasting time up here drinking coffee. He put his cup down, and his mind started spinning with confusion.

He wasn't about to blast out of here without a plan, though. Half the kids out there knew who he was. It wouldn't take long before Daniel would have him captured as another guest of honor. If he did get in, he couldn't just expose himself and demand Jada. He would have to blend in. If there was going to be a Black Mass, he would have to find a way to be part of it.

Marcus asked, "Does he know you?"

"He thinks I'm a joke trying to reform his captive audience."

He watched Grace when she answered. He thought she was too calm, but he realized he needed to slow down. He obviously had more at stake, but her rational approach would likely work out better. *I'll only have one chance down there...* He took back his coffee.

"We're two clowns in the same room." Marcus sat down at the table. "When's the last time you saw Jada?"

"When you guys left the church."

That seemed like such a long time ago to Marcus. When he left with Jada, she was only pregnant. That wasn't the best case, but it was at least normal. He had felt he was in control, but that feeling didn't last long. Soon after, every time he saw her she was bigger than the last. He never knew what to make of that, and he could tell Angelica had felt the same. He knew Angelica had been desperately trying to hold back her concerns, and that made Marcus nervous.

"Something's extremely wrong, Grace." He looked away shaking his head. "It's like she's gonna deliver anytime."

Hopelessness engulfed his face. So much had happened since then, he had almost forgotten about the pregnancy. Now it was ingrained, front and center, in his mind. He wondered if things had gotten worse. Maybe it was just a growth spurt. He stared at his coffee. *Probably not...* He sighed knowing he had to find her.

Grace held her cup tightly with both hands. "He's not normal you know," she said.

"I know. He seemed invincible when the church was burning."

He wasn't looking at Grace when he said that. He was watching the warm embrace she had, holding on to her cup. He saw her fingers loosen. The cup became isolated in thin air with nothing supporting it. As if in slow motion, it began to fall. He looked up and saw the shock on her face when it smashed.

"He was there?"

Marcus answered, "Yeah, why?"

She ignored the broken mess and moved quickly to the window that overlooked the alley. "Shit!" She turned back wildly to Marcus. "Shit, Marcus, he's ready! With the church gone he must be ready."

She said it as though Marcus knew exactly what she was talking about. Marcus looked all around, completely confused. *Ready for what?* He saw Louie open his eyes, irritated by the disturbance.

"The Black Mass is our only hope—our last hope. It's gotta end there," Grace continued.

Marcus was still shocked thinking he had missed something. "Ready for what?" He knew that came out barely audible, but Grace was ignoring him anyway.

"But once we're in, we won't get out."

Marcus could tell she said that to Louie, like he knew too. "What's he ready for, Grace?"

He watched Louie slowly sit up on the couch. If he did know, it didn't seem to bother him much. Or maybe he was just ready for anything. He was here after all. It was probably the last place he wanted to be, but he was here. He was ready to help his brother and ready to help the girl who tried to kill him… *Or was it the prospect of being able to claim the streets his own, his main motivator?*

"The way I go in, no one's gettin' out," Louie said.

"Yeah, just what we need. Rambo in hell," Grace replied.

"Well let me tell ya one thing, sweetheart, this fucker's not jumpin' in the fire pit without one hell of a water gun." Louie stood up and headed for the door. "I wonder who is open on Christmas Eve? Don't leave without me, bro. You'll thank me later."

It was like these two had suddenly decided what would go down next. They knew the result if they didn't act now, so doing it was just a formality. But the question for Marcus was still the same—what were they stopping?

Grace came to the table and sat down with Marcus. "I'll be a lit up tree if I go in there."

"What's he ready for, Grace?" She was thinking, still ignoring his question.

"Unless I have a black robe."

He watched her rush to a closet and quickly look through some clothes. A robe will make her one of them, he thought. He needed the same thing. For the next while, Marcus needed to abandon Christianity and become a Satanist. He felt he could do that to save his child and its mother, but still, he needed to know what Grace knew.

"Grace—"

She turned back to the table, but Marcus was right in front of her.

"I just need to get—"

"Grace, stop!" He paused making sure he had her full attention. "Ready for what?" he demanded.

Grace hesitated. She blinked rapidly then started nodding.

"You don't know about any of this do you?"

Marcus knew she didn't need an answer. She rushed back to the table and picked up a remote. She turned on a small TV. The menu of a DVD hard drive displayed. All the thumbnails showed some type of political event. She played the first one.

International leaders posed for many flashing cameras. Another showed the President during an address to the nation. Then there was a group shot during a G4 summit. In the background of each clip was Daniel—well groomed and high profile.

"To claim victory against good? To free evil from the gates of hell?" She paused and closed her eyes. "To create world domination for Satan."

"Really, Grace? Seems a bit over the top don't ya think?" *So much for her being the calm one.* He watched her shake her head.

"The church was his when you were not there, or any other priest for that matter. He makes his plans there, but he's failed in the past. Now the church is gone. The way I see it, this is his last chance."

"So what does he want with Jada?"

"At first you were in the way, because you occupied the church. He used her to get to you. Now, it's because of something else."

She looked at him, obviously not wanting to say anymore. He didn't need to hear it either. There was a baby involved.

He knew they both were fully aware of that.

"And Louie knows all of this?"

"Everyone knows bits and pieces. They know his influences and connections. They all fear his capabilities. I've just been taking notes."

He watched her run quickly for the door.

"Stay here, Marcus."

In an instant, she was gone. Louie had already left. Now, Marcus was alone but for how long? He couldn't just sit here waiting for who knows what.

He watched the clip still playing. He got up and slowly walked to the window. The kids were still out there. He looked down into the alley. He saw the door he burst out from with Jada. It had no handle, just a lock.

CHAPTER 50

MARCUS WAS ON THE SAME STREET he had been on when he followed Jada. He had made it out of Grace's apartment and through the hordes of goth kids unnoticed. This area was away from all of them, but just barely. He came here hoping to find exactly what he did. There was no sign of life, death, or anything in between. It made him feel isolated and too far away from Daniel's festivities, but he'd been here before. He knew this could get him into that satanic underworld. Regardless of whether it was the back door or the grand entrance, it made no difference. At this point, he had no other choice.

As he checked the area carefully, he realized the word of a Black Mass must have had an effect on both sides—good and evil. He looked into the doorway where he had hid. Next to that, he saw the figure of a man behind a store window watching him. A blind closed in an overhead apartment.

Apparently, the rest of the community knew exactly how to act when Daniel called the kids to the street. They did nothing to get in the way. All they did was hide.

He walked toward the corner then stopped. At least he was alone, he thought. No one had confronted him as the priest from St. Paul's. No one tried to help by getting him off the street. He was being ignored just like all of Daniel's past actions had. He looked to the dead end, and beyond, then to the alley that led to the stairway.

Marcus approached the stairs with caution, stopping before making the commitment to go down. He knew that once he was in, there would be no turning back. He considered doing what everyone else did. While standing here in silence and looking down at a place he may never return from, he could see some logic in that—look out for number one… He didn't have to be the hero. He didn't have to save everyone who didn't care a bit about him. They hadn't reacted to his offerings as a priest, so why should he risk everything for them. He thought about it for a second, but the answer was simple for Marcus. Especially after everything he'd been through. He had come here to make a difference, and now was his opportunity to do exactly that.

The silence was shattered with the crash of an industrial garbage lid. He spun around seeing the container but nothing else. The noise had been loud enough for it to be more than just random movement. His feeling of solitude was suddenly gone. Now he knew curious eyes were on him. He looked back to the stairway when suddenly, a red and black blur crashed into him. He lost his balance but held on to his attacker as they both tumbled down the stairway.

***

OTHER hooded figures passed as Marcus stood alone. The fight outside had been vicious, but Marcus was still street worthy. He simply did what he had to do, fast. He looked closely at the red and black robe he wore that was embroidered with symbols of Satan.

He saw what he thought must have been high priests sitting in front of an altar. They were more decorated than he was, but he appeared to be wearing the robe of a higher rank than others. Everyone waited quietly. It was obvious to Marcus that he was now part of this highly anticipated satanic ritual with no one the wiser.

An usher wearing a black robe approached and offered to lead him to a viewing place. At first he was reluctant, but he realized quickly his resistance would be stupid. He followed the unsuspecting usher which confirmed he had not been identified. Now that Marcus was inside, he was determined to blend in the best he could. Despite what he saw here, there would be no excuse for any heroism until the time was right. For now, Marcus would just watch, not really knowing how much his eyes could actually take.

The area quickly filled with satanic priests surrounding the ballroom floor. The sound of their movement filled the room, but no words were spoken. He wasn't sure where he should be, so he had to assume the usher knew where to place him from the symbols on his robe. So far, no curious eyes watched him. No one seemed to find him out of place. He knew that could change any second, but for now he seemed fine, so he stayed exactly where he was.

He noticed two groups, dressed in black robes, walking slowly from each side of the room. They circled along the back wall chanting.

"Hail, Satan, Lord of Darkness. King of Hell. Ruler of the Earth. God of this World."

They stopped at the middle of the back wall. From the darkness behind them, Daniel appeared. He led a group which Marcus assumed to include a deacon, another who seemed to be his subordinate, and two nuns. Daniel was the most decorated of all. Marcus once again, admired his majesty. His elaborate chasuble; the stole around his neck; a maniple over his left arm; his long, braided girdle around his waist defined him as the leader, without question.

Marcus quickly snapped out of this envy. He realized he had the same presence within Christianity. It was just the followers he missed. If he continued to lead, persistent in his goals, worshippers would find him. But these people were following Daniel, and Marcus knew that alone made him far more powerful.

In the middle of the group, Marcus saw Jada. She wore a long, flowing black garment. This time, however, it was not a slave. Instead, it controlled her. She seemed to only be participating with fear and uncertainty—terrorized as the center of attention. She obviously had no choice in her position within the group or the direction she walked. They moved through the priests with one group of ushers in front, the other behind.

Marcus twitched nervously but didn't dare leave where he stood. He continued to watch Daniel approach the high priests. Daniel instructed Jada to sit in a chair that was part of the altar. He drank from a chalice handed to him by one of the ushers. He passed it to the deacon.

Marcus was fascinated by what he saw. Daniel seemed to be copying the same ritual he used in a mass. He had never studied the procedures of a Black Mass, but this was definitely based on the faith that threatened Daniel the most. He didn't understand the logic behind that, but the process was riveting to him just the same.

Daniel motioned with both his hands to the floor at Jada's feet. As he raised his hands, the garment she wore rose. It completely lifted over her head and floated away behind her. The thought of this being similar to a Catholic mass was suddenly gone for Marcus. At the same time, it made Marcus nervous to see Jada there as vulnerable as she was. She sat naked but ornamented with oversized cosmetic jewelry, heavy makeup, and six inch stilettos. Body painted across her breasts was 666.

A bell began to ring. That broke the tension for Marcus, but two nuns immediately tended to Jada which brought his nervousness back. Marcus had thought for a second the attention on Jada would switch to something else, but he was wrong. It only intensified as the nuns made sure her legs were spread and that she grasped a candle holder in each hand.

Marcus had lost focus on Daniel, but Daniel hadn't gone anywhere. He took the chalice from the deacon and placed it between Jada's legs.

The high priests stood in front of her and bowed once.

"In nomine dei nostri Satanas Luciferi ad altare dei nostril," Daniel said.

"Ad dei nostri, Satanas Luciferi, qui laetificat juventutem meam," the deacons continued in unison.

Marcus's desire to learn more about this faith compelled him to continue watching, but he had to figure out what he would do when the Satanists decided to take this too far. He looked at the door he entered from. Again, it was gone. The place was rigged for all these illusions, he thought. He had convinced himself of that, but he felt the need to at least consider that it was all real. *If it is actually magic that Daniel possesses, how in God's name do I stand a chance against that?*

"Judicare, dues mess. Et discern—," Daniel continued.

Marcus was aware of the service going on in Latin, but trying to figure what was being said didn't concern him. Instead, he watched the ushers still lining the back wall, anticipating their next instruction. He looked among them for the weakest one then to the other side of the room. He tried to find a flaw or a missing link. Unfortunately, this place was wrapped up as tight as the drug labs he used to deliver packages to.

"Quia tu es Diabolus, foritudo mea," replied the deacons.

"I confess to all Lords of Hell—"

Marcus could find nothing vulnerable from where he was. He had to move.

"Our highest, most sacred leader. King of Hell, Satan; to Ishtar, our fertile God; to Amon, lord of life and reproduction—"

While the ritual continued, Marcus cautiously moved away from where he stood. He was careful not to attract any attention. He approached the back wall. Immediately, an usher stepped forward to assist. Marcus tried to brush him away, but the usher insisted on escorting him to another area.

The deacons continued, "I ask the almighty Satan to shower you with his blessings—"

Marcus didn't resist. He feared the disturbance if he did. He looked at the ushers he passed, slightly able to see their faces under draping hoods. Suddenly, he stopped and looked straight ahead. Something he'd just seen was not right. He didn't know exactly what it was, but it paralyzed him.

"Gratia tibi, fratres," Daniel said.

The usher turned back and motioned for Marcus to keep moving. Marcus stared straight at him but didn't move. *That last face...* He started to look back but stopped when the usher escorting him invited him to take another spot.

The entire congregation bowed as Daniel turned to them. Marcus reluctantly followed, but he was distracted by what confused him.

"I ask the undeniable King of Hell to fulfill your life wishes and help you in your selfishness of obtaining all your desires," Daniel said.

When Marcus stood up straight, he looked back to the ushers. He saw no faces, but one usher nodded. Marcus turned away as if he'd been discovered. *Was he nodding at me or to someone else? Possibly to Daniel about me...*

He narrowed his eyes in on the ceremony. He had to appear focused. His actions were beginning to be a dead giveaway. He watched an usher present a pot to one of the nuns. With great spectacle, she lifted her gown and urinated into it. She smiled with artificial pleasure. Marcus was shocked by what he was witnessing, but the usher was still distracting his thoughts. He tried to convince himself the nod was intended for him.

He continued to watch the deacon take the pot and pour urine into the chalice between Jada's legs.

Daniel held the pot up to the high priests sitting in front of him. He kissed it before aggressively showering the priests with leftover urine.

Marcus was confused by the spectacle in front of him and what might be going on around him. He worried that the usher was nodding to someone else. Could they be planning his exposure while he did nothing? Meanwhile, he just stood there watching Jada being manipulated and humiliated. All of this pushed him to his limits, but he knew the time wasn't right.

He sighed to calm himself while the deacon took the chalice, moved it slowly to his mouth then took a small drink. He passed it to the subdeacon who did the same. Marcus was aware of what he witnessed, but it didn't shock him as much as it should have. The thought of being exposed during all of this disturbed him much more.

Finally, he watched the chalice being passed to Daniel. He held it up to the Sigil of Baphomet, with a large inverted cross directly over its face. It proudly hung on the wall behind the altar. Daniel kissed the chalice and passionately took a drink himself.

He turned to Jada who showed obvious reluctance. Daniel moved to her holding the chalice in front of him. He held it to her lips. Marcus watched her close her eyes. She opened her mouth slightly, slowly.

Daniel lifted the chalice and intentionally missed her mouth. Urine poured onto her neck then ran between her breasts, onto her stomach and between her legs.

Daniel yelled, "Shemhamforash!"

"Shemhamforash!" the deacons repeated.

Daniel continued, "Hail, Satan!"

"Hail, Satan!"

The congregation became increasingly restless as Daniel continued in prayer. Marcus's eyes bulged. He looked all around. He didn't feel confined to stay completely still anymore. Others around him weren't. He felt relief as the built-up tension suddenly rushed out of him. He turned to confront the usher who had nodded to him. Within the shadow of the hood, Louie smiled back.

Daniel said, "We beg of thee, powerful Prince of Darkness, by the merits—"

Suddenly, Marcus began coughing, startling those around him. Louie was immediately at his side, helping him away from the other priests.

The distraction seemed to have gone off unnoticed since Marcus could hear Daniel continue. In the aisle, Marcus stayed bent over while Louie leaned to him. "Enjoying the show? I'm pissed you left without me," Louie said quietly.

Marcus ignored the humor. "Along the wall, there are doors. You can't see them, but they're there," he said while continuing his coughing fit. He put his arm around Louie for help to straighten up Their faces were inches from each other. "Neither of us moves until we have a way out."

Marcus broke away and returned to the priests. He was calmer now, but he was no further ahead. He still had to come up with a plan to get Jada out of here, but he did have Louie with him. That alone gave him confidence he had not felt before.

He continued watching Daniel who was now cleansing the altar with burning incense. Smoke surrounded Jada while she watched him like a child who feared being punished.

An usher smashed a mallet against a gong displayed off to the side. He hit it another time, then another.

Daniel took a small vial from the altar and removed a piece of communion bread. Marcus recognized it instantly—a host. *Did he get it from the church?* The thought of Daniel violating his sacred communion offering insulted and angered him. The thought of Daniel stealing it from under his nose made him feel like a failure.

Daniel showed the congregation then proceeded to pulverize it in a wooden bowl with a pestle, showing his anger and vengeance. He took some of the remains in his fingers and turned to Jada. With the passion of demons, he thrust his hand into Jada's crotch. He proceeded to stimulate her, although only he seemed to be aroused.

Marcus stirred and held himself back from busting into a screaming act of heroism. He knew it would be the end if he intervened. All eyes were on Daniel and they would be on him if he couldn't control himself. If he had a plan it would be different, but having nowhere to go after Jada was with him was simply a risk not worth taking.

Jada grasped tightly on to the candle holders. She turned away from Daniel and toward Marcus. For a moment, Marcus thought she saw him. He suddenly convinced himself she knew he was there. Maybe this was the right time, he thought. He looked around quickly, but something still didn't feel right. He struggled to figure out what seemed off, then he realized it was Jada. She didn't see him. She was just desperately looking for help from anyone. He knew that when she pleaded with a group of priests close by. He watched them ignore her and laugh at her cries.

His attention went back to Daniel as he finished with her. The deacon poured wine on his fingers that dripped into the bowl. A mixture of charcoal and incense was added and it was all lit on fire with the only white candle present among a sea of burning, black candles.

The deacon drove the mallet into the gong and continued

with repetition and aggression.

Marcus turned to move away again. He was frustrated with himself for simply watching and doing nothing. He had lost consciousness of those around him until someone bumped into him. It was Louie.

"Don't blow it, Father."

Marcus looked into his eyes and could tell Louie was determined to see this through to the end. He thought Louie was likely finding this entertaining. He didn't give a shit about Jada. Marcus forced himself to turn back while the continuous sound of the gong excited the audience further.

Daniel addressed the priests while pointing to Jada. "Bear witness to the fact that she carries the child of a Christian priest." He turned to Jada. "A feeble attempt at Christ's second coming?" He circled her with a vulture's stare—a look that said it all.

Marcus's head stopped spinning. He stared directly at Daniel. *What did you say? How would you know that or even think it?* But it did make some kind of sense. What else could explain the rapid pregnancy? And by the look on Jada's face, delivery could be anytime. Marcus knew Daniel had no intention to let that happen.

With Louie right there, the moment was now. Sure Louie didn't care about Jada, but he did care about Marcus. Marcus surged toward Daniel.

Louie held him back and pulled him out from the priests. He slammed him against the wall, startling those close by.

Marcus was only concerned about Jada, not those around

him. They appeared to be convinced, however, that this usher had the disruptive priest under control. He looked beyond them to Daniel who was too far away to notice the disturbance. He simply addressed the audience again.

"I am not just another lonely soul who walks the streets of Satan."

Marcus pushed Louie away as others turned back to Daniel. He watched Daniel raise his arms. The subdeacon removed the girdle from around his waist.

"I am not just another voice for lost youth to follow," Daniel said.

The subdeacon took the maniple from his left arm. Everyone around Marcus seemed to have already forgotten his outbreak.

"I am not just another leader of those who cannot lead themselves," Daniel continued.

His stole was removed from around his neck. Marcus looked to Louie, but he was lost in the moment just like the others.

"I am the chosen one. Chosen by Satan to spread his word. Chosen by Satan to spill the blood he desires," Daniel said.

His chasuble flew open exposing his nakedness and huge, bony wings that spread with relaxing fury.

The congregation gasped. Louie stepped back into Marcus. Marcus stopped him. He held him as he watched the unbelievable happening. Daniel suddenly grew to match his huge wingspan. He began to rise. A slight movement sent him soaring throughout the ballroom.

"A destiny as the Son of Satan," Daniel concluded.

Marcus walked slowly back into the group of priests as if suddenly in a trance from this fantastic sight. He forgot about Louie being there. He was fascinated, mesmerized. He was fixated on the beauty of this creature he despised.

Daniel swooped down on the priests. All of them were shocked by the unveiling truth. They cheered at the site of Daniel's majesty.

Marcus ducked as Daniel barely cleared the top of his head. He felt like cheering too, but looked away instead. He took a deep breath and looked back for Louie. He ran to him. "Where's Grace?"

Louie was stunned too, still watching.

"Louie! Where's Grace?"

Marcus looked up while Daniel circled high within the ceiling of the ballroom.

"I am his blood. I am his body and soul!"

He landed in front of Jada, tucked in his wings, and returned to normal height. Marcus shook Louie while he continued watching Daniel. Daniel addressed the priests.

"I am your leader in our quest for world domination." He hissed at Jada. "Be honored that I am your executioner."

Marcus shook Louie harder, snapping him out of his fascination. Marcus dashed into the aisle, frantically looking for a way out. He looked to see if Louie was following him. Louie was watching him, but he hadn't moved. Marcus ran back to him "Grace, Louie! Where is she?"

"She's here somewhere, but I ain't lookin' for her," Louie replied.

Marcus watched Louie turn and open his robe slightly.

"Huntin' season just opened, brother."

He showed Marcus a semi-automatic pistol he had strapped to his side.

"Told ya you'd thank me."

Marcus saw Daniel motion to the deacons. They each took Jada by the arm as she screamed and struggled to get away. She fell to the ground and scurried to Daniel's feet.

"Please, Daniel, your highness, Son of Satan. Please forgive me for my sins against you."

He ignored her. The deacons secured her again. A nun placed a black cape around Daniel's shoulders. The other nun held the garment Jada had worn. She threw it over Jada's head. The garment engulfed her.

Daniel looked to the back of the room. Marcus looked there too as two ushers swung adjoining doors open exposing a dark tunnel. Daniel walked toward it with the deacons following, one carrying a sword that was displayed next to the gong.

Marcus saw Jada fighting for her life. He panicked knowing this would be his only chance. He looked frantically in all directions. He saw priests, and ushers; but not Louie. He was too flustered to be able to focus.

"A sacrifice will occur in the Palace of Satan after which we will celebrate with this, my gift of a priest's child to my father," Daniel announced.

Marcus rushed for the doors as Jada was being led toward them. Ushers instantly swarmed him.

Marcus helplessly watched Daniel, already at the doors. He left through them. Marcus saw the deacons follow with Jada under their control. She pleaded with whomever she passed, but they all ignored her. She was pushed through the doors, one of which was shut immediately. The other remained open by an usher.

Marcus was being pulled away, but he remained focused on the doors. It seemed odd that one would remain open. He looked back for Louie who was running toward him. He pulled out the pistol and fired a shot into the ceiling.

The ushers, holding Marcus, were distracted by the shot. Others panicked.

Louie continued toward Marcus with all eyes on him. Marcus saw a priest attack him from behind. Louie turned quickly and took out whomever was there with three shots.

Marcus freed himself. He looked to the door which was still open, held by an usher—another intruder, disguised. He yelled, "Go Grace!"

He saw a group starting to approach her. He looked back to Louie who was fighting off his attackers. Louie fired two more shots and plowed his way to Marcus.

Marcus saw Grace surrounded. She moved into the tunnel and pushed on the door to keep it open.

Louie grabbed Marcus's arm, swinging him into motion.

Marcus watched others attacking the door as Grace desperately fought back.

Louie fired. Two ushers dropped. He pushed Marcus who slid through the opening. Marcus surged back for Louie as he fired randomly until the magazine was empty. Louie turned to the door, smashing anyone in his way. He got through and slammed it shut.

CHAPTER 51

MARCUS LEANED WITH HIS BACK against the door. His eyes were closed as he struggled to catch his breath. He opened them slowly. It was dark, wet, and quiet in the underground tunnel.

Louie and Grace were right there. How long would it be before they were not alone, Marcus thought? He wanted to preserve this peacefulness for as long as he could, but they had to keep moving. Daniel had Jada somewhere in here, and he knew others were not far away.

Louie asked, "Everyone good?"

Marcus watched him light a lighter, release the empty magazine from the gun, and replace it with a new one. He looked at Grace watching in awe. She seemed to feel the same as he did. He was amazed that Louie didn't appear phased at all from what went on in there. Years on the streets created this cold hearted soul he had for a brother. *But what would I have done without him?*

Louie looked up at both of them. He removed his robe revealing the holster he wore. Grace did the same which exposed a knife she had attached around her waist. Louie reached into his pocket and threw Marcus a pocket knife. Marcus looked at it with disgust. He fired a glance back with a shake of his head and a half smile.

Louie shrugged and smiled. "Don't worry." He looked at his gun. "I wanna see the Son of Satan suck on the end of this mother fucker. Let's go."

Go where, Marcus thought to himself but didn't say anything. Daniel and his followers could be anywhere in this maze. They would know these paths, but outsiders... He doubted Louie or Grace knew them. He hoped they did, but he really wished they didn't. At this point, Marcus had no interest in finding out that either of them were somehow wrapped up in the likes of Daniel. He knew Louie was right, though. They couldn't just stand there looking at each other. They had to go, now.

When Marcus pushed himself away from the door, Grace turned, shocked to see that she had a rat cornered. She swiftly took her knife, and without hesitation, Louie grabbed her arm.

"He's okay," Louie said with his eye on the rat.

He nudged it gently with his foot giving it a quick getaway. Marcus watched him look calmly at Grace then take off down a long passage.

Marcus pushed the robe off his shoulders. He followed

with Grace next to him. At first he was fine with letting Louie lead the way. He was armed the best, and he definitely was operating in his element. The only thing was, having him in front left him an open target. He was sure Grace wouldn't object to that, but he did. This whole mess was his problem, and Louie was his younger brother. He surged forward to catch up to him.

Ahead, light shone into the tunnel from a sewer cover near the top of the ceiling. As they got closer, Marcus noticed water pouring in. He could hear the rumbling of thunder from a storm and rushing water that had gathered to this spot. The water down here followed a crevasse in the floor that ran off in another direction. Marcus's instinct was to follow the water, but he had no idea if that was the right way to go. By the looks of it, he wouldn't be making the decision anyway. Louie was still in front.

Louie was the first to jump over the crevasse, but the echo of him landing startled bats that lined the walls. Screeching and flapping wings flooded the tunnel as though they were attacking Louie, but Marcus realized the bats were only trying to get away. Louie ducked and fell to the ground while they flew over top of him.

Marcus noticed Grace looking down the sewer where the water flowed. She appeared to be thinking the same as Marcus.

"We should go this way," she said.

Louie got up and threw a stiletto to Marcus. "Guess it's past midnight." He continued in the direction the bats took.

CHAPTER 52

A SLIGHTLY OPENED OLD, wooden door was up ahead. Marcus knew where it would lead as soon as he saw it, and the fact it was opened told him he didn't get here first. He rushed past the other two and pushed it open into the basement room in the church. It was infested with bats.

He hadn't been in this room much, but he knew it had always been empty. Now that it was decorated with bats, it took on a whole new look. His entrance disturbed them. They suddenly swarmed the air and escaped into the basement hallway.

Marcus followed, running through the hallway then up the stairs to the foyer. Bats flooded the sky that was completely exposed from the fire. Rain and wet snow poured into the destroyed area as thunder rumbled in the distance. This fantastic sight didn't get much of Marcus's attention because no one was here. Instead, Marcus looked ahead to the church.

Daniel came back here. Marcus knew that. Even though it was destroyed and there was nothing left for either of them, Daniel was here to perform his final act against Jada and the baby. After that, who knew what he had planned.

Before Marcus took a step forward, he looked again at the destruction all around him. It didn't matter whose side occupied it, this building was the single thing that kept these two faiths at war. Now, only one would prevail. It had taken well over a hundred years to get to this point, but now was the moment it all came down to. Marcus shook his head realizing how incredible it was to truly understand the power of wood, brick, and mortar.

Louie and Grace came up from behind him. He knew they were there, but Marcus was fixated on the church again. He started to walk through the foyer toward the main aisle.

What was once classic and beautiful, now was completely destroyed. Burnt, demolished—a perfect temple for the beast that occupied the sanctuary.

Marcus watched from the main aisle as Daniel stood over top of Jada who was lying on what was left of the altar. The deacons flanked him. They seemed to admire him while he had one hand concealed under his cape that moved in the rhythmic motion of a man masturbating.

"Dear, Lord Satan, we pray that you honor us with all evil, past, present, and future," a deacon said.

Louie quietly moved toward a side aisle and motioned for Grace to take the other.

"And fulfill us with all our desires so that we will be forever free to sin," the subdeacon said.

Marcus stayed where he was. "Even destroyed, God will not allow Satan, or his son, into his house." He said it calmly and quietly as if convincing himself, but his voice carried within the charred remains.

The deacons turned to him, shocked that they had been exposed. One held the sword that he instantly waved to display the power he possessed by having it.

Daniel stopped his obscene presentation of self-pleasure. He turned away from Jada with anger and arrogance. He bolted forward while his wings disrobed him. He flew directly at Marcus.

"This palace has never been a house of God," he commanded.

Marcus ducked when a shot rang out from the side aisle. It missed Daniel and smashed a stained glass window. Marcus could see how much it distracted Daniel. He soared into the space of the church with rain pouring in. Even though Louie missed, the shot could have been enough to save his life right there, Marcus thought. Marcus kept his eyes on Daniel as he landed on top of an incinerated beam.

"The father has come to see the birth of his child, even in death. How touching," Daniel said.

Marcus began to move quickly down the aisle. "A birth, yes, but you'll be killing me before you touch my child."

The deacon with the sword moved in front of Jada.

"My intention, exactly," Daniel said.

Another shot fired, but this time it hit the sword and was immediately followed by another that lodged into the side of the deacon's head.

The subdeacon reacted, but he was cut down by a blade slicing into his throat. Grace stepped away from behind him as he sunk to the ground. She wiped her blade clean and quickly went to Jada.

Marcus saw Louie taking aim at Daniel. He took another shot. This time it hit, slicing Daniel's thigh wide open. Blood poured from the wound, and Daniel launched into flight with a howling, ghostly scream. He soared through the collapsed roof as a bolt of lightning struck and thunder echoed within the burnt ruins.

Marcus rushed to Jada who was being moved by Grace beside the bell that lay in the destroyed tower. He turned quickly back to Louie. He was walking slowly toward them as if his job was done. But it wasn't, and Marcus could see why from high within the roofs opening. He began to yell at Louie, but his words didn't come out fast enough.

Daniel swooped down, back into the church. Marcus surged toward Louie but tripped into a pile of fallen beams. Daniel picked Louie up with a foot that had turned into a talon. He flew over Marcus with Louie helplessly being attacked by the other talon.

Shots were being fired, but they had no intended target. Daniel left through the roof. Louie was his prey.

Marcus recovered. He stumbled over the burnt debris to get back to Jada and Grace.

He stopped short of touching Jada when he saw her face full of stress and pain. It was obvious that contractions had taken over.

Marcus stood shocked, not knowing what to do. Suddenly, Daniel reappeared from the hole in the wall caused by the fallen bell tower. He swooped back into the destruction, straight at them. He let Louie's lifeless body crash beside Marcus.

Marcus fell desperately to save his brother but realized it was too late. He looked to Jada who was continuing to struggle in imminent labor. He looked up, unable to control any of this. This was his church. This was where he should be able to come for help. This was his future, but everything was gone now.

In the main aisle, he saw Daniel crouched down, poised, and ready for action. His wings were relaxed, and his fists were firmly planted on the ground between his bent legs.

"Who goes first? The priest or his savior?"

"This baby is God's will, and the miracle of its creation will also be the miracle of your demise," Marcus said.

"My demise will not come from a child nor any other power you possess."

Marcus stood his ground protecting Jada as Daniel began to grow. He descended upon Marcus.

"Only my powers will have any effect on life or death," Daniel said.

Marcus turned away as Jada screamed in pain. Grace was with her, but she cowered under the presence of Daniel's massive existence.

Jada screamed again. Marcus went to help her, leaving the inevitable confrontation with Daniel. She pushed, noticing Marcus beside her.

Marcus looked up. The rain continued to pour down, but a beam of daylight appeared from the wall behind them. He noticed Daniel now over top of them, then suddenly, a gust of wind pushed him back. The skies beyond the wall opened up and wind continued to blow forcing Daniel away, despite his size.

Jada pushed again. She strained under the force of her contraction. Another push and the baby was born into Grace's hands.

Marcus watched Daniel fighting the wind and the driving rain with persistence while sun brightened the sanctuary. He stood up, into the wind, facing Daniel in the aisle. "The powers that brought this life are not yours. It is the power of God." He turned to Grace and took the knife from his pocket. He sliced the umbilical cord with urgency. He took the baby in his arms.

He smiled as the sun shone brightly, directly on them. He turned back to Daniel. "As you are the Son of Satan, she is the daughter of our Heavenly Father," Marcus said. He held the baby up to face Daniel. "And then that lawless one will be revealed, whom the Lord will slay with the breath of her mouth and bring to an end by the appearance of her coming."

Again, the wind blew, rain pounded, and the sun shone on

the baby, reflecting into Daniel's eyes. Marcus watched the ground in front of him begin to break away as though an earthquake had struck. A deep crevasse formed, creating a barrier between him and Marcus. "This is God's will. These are God's words."

More earth broke away, exposing jagged rocks, boiling water, and burning canyons with no endings.

Marcus continued, "And this is God's church!"

Marcus saw Daniel looking into his cherished Hell then back to Marcus. As the ground beneath him gave away, his breathtaking wingspan lifted him effortlessly.

Lightning struck; thunder cracked. One of Daniel's wings received a direct hit. He began to fall despite his spastic attempts to do otherwise. Marcus watched with the baby in his arms. Uncontrollably, Daniel crashed into the crevasse that closed up as fast as it formed.

The wind and rain stopped. The sun continued to shine as Marcus turned back to Jada. He looked at his daughter. "Almighty and ever living God, you send us this child to cast out the power of Satan, spirit of evil. We pray for her and name her, Christina, in honor of your son, Jesus Christ." He touched her ears and mouth with his thumb then handed her to Jada.

He looked for Louie. At first he had trouble finding him and thought he wasn't dead, but that was just wishful thinking. Louie's body had settled into a collection of ashes. Marcus looked at him thinking his burial had already begun.

He took another look around the church. The crevasse

was gone, but the destruction remained. He knew the church could never be restored again.

CHAPTER 53

MARCUS STOOD BESIDE A PLAQUE that was mounted on a waist high, stone pillar. He glanced at it, satisfied with the results after searching long and hard for this display that had to be exactly the way he'd envisioned it. It read: "*St. Paul's Roman Catholic Church. In memory of Father Davis Burke.*"

He looked up to the sun shining down on his newly constructed, modern church. He could hear the choir inside singing. He smiled at people passing by him and entering the large double doors of the main entrance. He stayed there for a moment after the last person made his way in. He looked out at this totally revitalized neighborhood that was no longer beaten beyond recovery. It did recover, and Marcus had been primarily the reason why.

He considered the drastic turn things had taken since his showdown with Daniel. These people had always been looking for someone to lead them, he thought. He didn't blame them for taking the wrong path. They had just chosen greed and corruption as the most appealing option. Now their choice was with him, and he fully intended to serve them well—something they had not experienced in an extremely long time.

A smiling, young couple rushed up the walkway. They were late but determined to make it before anything started. Marcus's patience calmed them. He let the couple enter the opened doors before entering himself. He took one last look outside and closed the doors.

***

INSIDE, Marcus stood behind the altar in his all saints silk chasuble. He looked to the choir as they were finishing their opening hymn. He never had a choir at the old church. The organ had been a classic. It had been well worth preserving, but he thought he liked the choir best. It was made up of real people—people who cared about making a difference too. They also knew all the songs, so Marcus didn't have to worry about writing any. He smiled to himself remembering that first meeting with Father Burke. He continued smiling while he watched the choir during their last note.

Marcus began, "In the name of the Father, and of the Son, and of the Holy Spirit." He made the sign of the cross.

"Amen," the congregation responded.

"May the grace and peace of God our Father and the Lord

Jesus Christ be with you," Marcus said.

Among the congregation, he saw Jada sitting in the front pew with Christina in her arms.

"And also with you," he could hear her say with a smile.

Grace sat beside her. On her other side, Angelica showed the pride she always had.

Behind them, rows of pews were completely filled with parishioners anxiously awaiting his comforting words. He had spent months working with new leaders in the community while this church was being built. They formed social groups and planned common interest gatherings. He knew they wanted to hear his message. Their faces were young. They didn't have the ceremony memorized, and best of all, no one was sleeping.

Marcus smiled at them, taking in the moment. He looked throughout the congregation then to Angelica, Jada, Christina, and Grace.

"Welcome, everyone, to St. Paul's Catholic Church. And welcome to a new beginning—a new hope and promise that we can all embrace." He took a vial from the altar that contained holy water. "Dear friends, this water will be used to remind us of our baptism. Let us ask God to bless it, and to keep us faithful to the spirit he has given us." He placed it back down on the altar and bowed his head to it. He took the vial and walked around the altar. "God our Father, your gift of water brings life and freshness to the earth." He moved along the aisle in front of the first pew, sprinkling the holy water on all of the people including Angelica, Jada, Christina, and Grace. "It washes away our sins and brings us eternal life."

He looked up to the congregation. Some were shocked as they looked beyond him. Marcus was confused by the sudden change of expressions. Someone let out a slight scream— holding it back like a muffled sneeze.

He spun around and saw a rat casually walking on the altar. It didn't seem to care that it was now the center of attention. It wasn't concerned about where it was, and it didn't show signs of going anywhere else. It saw Marcus and stood aggressively on its hind legs.

Unsure of what to do, Marcus grabbed his ceremonial stole from around his neck and cautiously approached it.

At first, the rat appeared perfectly fine to go one on one with Marcus; but as Marcus got closer, it squealed and scurried onto the floor, then between Marcus's legs.

Screaming started among the congregation. Marcus knew he had to do something, quick.

He watched it stop in front of Christina. It hissed then continued up Angelica's leg. It scurried across Jada's and Grace's laps.

Marcus stood frozen as parishioners fell over each other, trying to get away from it. It ran for the side door that was left open.

Marcus chased it. He stopped at the door. The rat was nowhere to be seen. He remembered leaving the door open to let the sunshine inside, but in hindsight, that was a bad idea. He closed his eyes, shaking his head slightly. He turned to go back inside.

As he closed the door, he saw a low riding, fully customized, foreign car moving slowly along the street with black metal hell pounding. The engine revved twice, and the car peeled away.

Marcus looked back to the congregation that was still in disarray. He saw Jada watching him with a cunning smile.

###

ABOUT THE AUTHOR

A FEW YEARS AGO I lost my job...

It had been because of corporate downsizing and bailouts; a financial crisis—however you want to look at it. Basically, though, it all had come down to the same thing. I'd lost a career that, up until that point, I'd spent my whole adult life doing. It was what I'd gone to school for. It gave me financial security. From it, I felt confidence when I asked my wife to marry me. We've had children. We've enjoyed a North American, middle class lifestyle. But suddenly, all I had seemed in jeopardy, because I'd lost my job...

Before this day, I had started writing. It had been years before that in fact, and I had completed many stories. Somehow, I had found the creativity within me that had been locked away from the dilemma of *life getting in the way*.

The stories I had written were screenplays. They had done okay in Hollywood. Some were *recommended;* they were *championed*, but none were *sold*. So I had found myself jobless with my pockets full of stories, and there was nothing to stop me from letting my creative freedom run wild. Remember, I'd lost my job, so what would I do while I looked for another? The answer was simple. Write—three new screenplays; all high concept; all budgeted to sell. When they were done, they were all *recommended* and *championed*. But none of them *sold*...

Soon after I'd completed that third screenplay, I got a new job. It was actually the same job I'd had before, because those who had let me go, called me back. I remember being amazed and relieved that I would once again receive financial reward for my efforts. My creativity, though, was about to get stuck in the same sinkhole it had been in before.

The new job had been challenging and involved a heavy workload. I was determined to excel and make a difference, but something had to go. There simply wasn't enough time in the day, so I stopped writing.

At first it didn't bother me. I hadn't been making any money at writing, and I was really just doing it for myself. I simply couldn't fit it into an already cramped life. After a while, however, my fingers needed to speak again.

I had found myself outlining another screenplay when I stopped and thought about it all. I had issues with two things. Few were reading my work, and no one was putting up the money so others could see it; but it didn't have to be that way, and I finally figured out that I shouldn't be writing screenplays.

Purified, my debut novel, had been born from that

thinking. After I published *Purified*, I moved straight into writing *Sins of a Priest*. Now I realize that writing is something I'm not going to be able to get away from. It's in me, and it must come out. I recently read a quote from Steve Harvey's book, *Act Like a Success, Think Like a Success*: "*Our creator, in his infinite wisdom, created every single soul with a gift. When we utilize our gift, the universe thanks us by giving us an abundance of riches.*"

I'm writing this on the first day after I've lost my job, again... By taking away what I've conveniently become dependent on, the opportunity to write more has once again been put in front of me. Is this happening because I've found my *gift*? Is writing novels the *gift* I'm supposed to be giving to you?

Of course, only time will tell. The push and pull of my needs and desires will inevitably determine a winner. But after handing in my company assigned laptop and accepting that my key card is now powerless, there's one thing I know for sure...

I'm not jobless. I'm a writer.

CPSIA information can be obtained at www.ICGtesting.com
Printed in the USA
LVOW11s2110040215

425739LV00001B/8/P